A tornado whips through a community tossing about houses, furniture, cars, trees, and people like confetti.

Vicious rain causes a  banks. A dike collapses. stranded, and farmland is i

A hurricane sends an .... of soil and water careening down a mountain slope, taking everything in its way: houses, trees, large rocks, small bridges, automobiles, livestock, railroads.

A fire sweeps through the business section of a city.

The earth heaves under its burdensome load, toppling buildings, crumpling highways, and splitting mountains.

Within hours Mennonite Disaster Service (MDS) is on the scene with unpaid volunteers ready to help bring order out of chaos. What motivates this unusual organization (with a paid staff of one!) that has won commendation from the President of the United States and is recognized by Congress as a key voluntary agency alongside Red Cross and the Salvation Army?

This book tells how an idea that was born at a Mennonite picnic in Kansas twenty-five years ago has mushroomed into an international force for constructive help to those in sudden need.

Day of Disaster

Katie Funk Wiebe

Introduction by
Senator Birch Bayh

HERALD PRESS
Scottdale, Pennsylvania
Kitchener, Ontario

The following photos are from the MDS files of MCC: pages 19; 25 (Don Ziegler); 43 and 65 (Burton Buller); 69 (Don Ziegler); 77 (Leland Gerber); 111; 123 (Phil Diller); 135 (Burton Buller); 143 (Jan Swartzendruber); 171 (Gayle Koontz); and 181 (Fred Steiner). The photos on pages 35, 57, 99, and 103 are by Richard Blosser, used by permission of *Mennonite Weekly Review*. The photo on page 63 is from *The Washington Post*.

First Printing, February 1976
Second Printing, April 1976

Dedicated to every man, woman, and young person who, as an MDS volunteer, has at some time given his or her services to a person in need.

CONTENTS

PREFACE

I must confess. The idea to write a book about Mennonite Disaster Service (MDS) never grew in my mind like ideas for some books develop in the minds of their authors, sometimes over a period of years. Instead, it grew in the minds of individuals who had watched MDS grow from a small, unstructured organization to an international movement. They realized that many of the inspiring experiences of MDS volunteers were being lost, for no one was recording them. They heard many voices extolling the virtues of MDS, sometimes beyond what they thought it deserved. They heard other voices asking questions about MDS and knew that little had ever been published about MDS in a form which could be shared with such persons. They believed the time had come to gather the many experiences of MDSers in Canada and the United States so that more people could read the unique story of this growing volunteer movement.

Those who felt the need for a book to interpret MDS to the general public asked me to consider writing it. Why not? I had always had a secret desire to fathom the mystique of the MDS volunteer who willingly rises at dawn to spend a long, tiring day mucking out a smelly basement for no financial reward. What is his secret?

Also, as the child of Mennonite parents who migrated to Canada from Russia in 1923 and who escaped death by famine because of the kind intervention of American Mennonites, I look for opportunities to say thanks by writing about other people helping those in need.

When I began research, the question I was asked nearly every place I went was whether I was writing a history. The answer is still "No." This book is not a history. That still remains to be written. This book includes some historical sketches, but it represents my view of MDS from where I sit. I talked to interested persons and read newspaper accounts, published talks, and unpublished personal notes. MDSers are not known for keeping detailed written accounts of their experiences. This is understandable, but makes it difficult for a writer. *Day of Disaster* is an attempt to give the person who knows much and the person who knows little about MDS some fresh glimpses of a significant lay movement in contemporary times.

I must add that this book is not the complete picture. The stories included ` here must be considered as representative of hundreds of other similar experiences of MDSers in Canada and the United States. They could have been recorded also. Much material had to be omitted because of space limitations. I chose from the material I had the examples which I thought best typified the MDS experience.

By its very nature, the making of this book has been the affair of many people, especially the thousands of volunteers who continue to make MDS possible. In writing each chapter, I peered over the shoulders of others as they pointed out to me what they had seen and experienced. If the focus is not always clear, the problem may be that looking through two pairs of glasses at once tends to blur the image. If at times I have seen MDS too big, one reason is that the frequent retelling of stories changes even the darkest, dirtiest basement into a place of glory. And who would want to deny that caring can do that? If I have seen MDS too small, the reason is that each volunteer brings his humanity with him wherever he goes, and I may have caught too much of his humanness in that moment.

I particularly thank the following for their assistance: Syd Reimer who offered me anything of his I wanted related to MDS; Lois Barrett and Urie A. Bender, who did much of the research related to the history of MDS in the United States and Canada; Norman Wingert who gathered much of the material for the chapters on the overseas projects; Robert Kreider, through whose eyes I saw the annual meeting of MDSers; Marie Wiens; Marvin Hostetler and John Diller, veteran Kansas MDSers whose interest in having the story written encouraged me; Merle Herr, who provided material for the story on the Community Mennonite Fellowship in New York; and MDS and MCC personnel who read and edited the manuscript.

As I worked with the material, page by page, I found myself becoming increasingly proud to be a Mennonite. I present here a portrait of MDS, done in mosaic, which will never be completed as long as MDS continues to serve in the name of Christ.

Katie Funk Wiebe
October 1975

INTRODUCTION

On Palm Sunday in 1965 a series of vicious tornadoes ripped through northern Indiana and part of the adjoining states of Michigan and Illinois. The following week I was one of a group of Congressmen who flew out with the late President Johnson to inspect the damage and to provide what moral support we could to the unfortunate victims.

I'll never forget that scene as we surveyed the damage. The destruction was awesome. Those tornadoes had struck a cruel blow to the lives and hopes of many Hoosiers and other residents of the Midwest.

Although that tragedy was something I'll never forget, there was something else I'll always remember about that day. That was the sight of the many volunteers of Mennonite Disaster Service from Indiana and other states who were on the scene helping the dazed victims rebuild their shattered lives. In this hour of need, the Mennonites truly appeared to be heaven-sent.

From its beginnings more than twenty-five years ago as the Mennonite Service Organization, Mennonite Disaster Service has grown to become an international organization dedicated to providing help to disaster victims wherever it is needed.

Today the tradition of MDS continues as men and women, young and old unselfishly go where they are needed to pitch in to aid disaster victims.

Officials of MDS have also been a great help to disaster victims in another way—in our mutual search for the best way to provide and coordinate public and private disaster relief assistance. After those Palm Sunday tornadoes it was obvious to me that the federal government needed to follow the example of Mennonite

Disaster Service and establish a continuing mechanism to provide help for the innocent victims of any type of disaster.

With the help of MDS officials, and those witnesses who appeared before my Public Works Subcommittee, we were able to come up with the first comprehensive federal disaster relief legislation that directly helps victims and allows federal assistance to be dispensed through private organizations such as MDS.

Today, just as the various congregations that make up MDS are ready to help at a moment's notice, so is the federal government through the Federal Disaster Assistance Administration.

Mennonite Disaster Service has led the way in providing help, when it is so vitally needed, to their fellowmen. *Day of Disaster* tells on a very personal level of the many unsung contributions these volunteers have made.

It may be too soon to call MDS a legend, but the description of the sacrifices of MDS volunteers recorded here can only add to its outstanding reputation. The story of MDS is as unselfish as it is amazing. It is an inspiration to us all.

Birch Bayh, Indiana
United States Senator

Chapter One

MUD, MUCK,
AND MENNONITES

Rapid City is a great place to live and a great place to vacation. Built along the Rapid Creek on the edge of the Black Hills of South Dakota, the city nestles comfortably in the valley. The creek, normally a mild-flowing stream, winds lazily from the southwest side of the city to the southeast. Hundreds of visitors travel through Rapid City each year to camp and fish in the Black Hills, to visit the caves, and to gaze at the stony faces of four former Presidents carved in the granite on beautiful Mount Rushmore.

But the usual serenity of the area was grossly shattered on the evening of June 9, 1972.

A freakish weather pattern had brought up to fourteen inches of rain in the hills west of the city, the normal rainfall for an entire year. Runoff from the hills soon began pouring into Rapid Creek, causing it to push over its banks. By late afternoon motorists were driving through water a foot deep in the Black Hills, and storm clouds were moving east toward Rapid City.

As the rains became torrential, flood alerts went out to people living in the flood plains, but many shrugged it off. Minor flooding had occurred along the creek many springs.

The Canyon Lake Dam burst shortly before 11:00 p.m., sending a wall of water roaring along Rapid Creek. The seemingly harmless stream where fishermen waded and children splashed became a tide of devastating destruction.

In the pitch-black night, with rain falling in sheets, water charged down the mountain, dislodging houses, cars, trailers, and bridges as it rushed to its unknown destination. Giant trees were uprooted. Huge gouges marred the carefully manicured lawns and parks. Entire housing areas were swept away. Ruptures in gas lines added new hazards.

The water rose by the second and battered on doors and windows. Without waiting for admittance, it shattered the panes of glass and poured in. People raced to second floors, attics, rooftops, and trees. Yet the water followed them.

Escape by car was impossible for many. Some who tried never made it.

All we have to do is stay together and remain calm. Calm, yes, that's it. This house will never break away from its foundation. It's solid.

And then they saw it—an entire house bobbing past them. People they knew were clinging to the roof, screaming, wasting their waning strength competing with the roar of the enraged river.

Then they heard the cracking noise of timbers tearing loose under the growing force and weight of the water. They heard their own car smash through the garage wall and watched it spin out of sight. With a sucking noise the garage tumbled. Then the house rocked back and forth on its foundation before it finally broke loose also, pitching over on its side and dumping its riders into the greedy river.

Survivors related stories of hearing screaming voices throughout the night. They saw friends and neighbors struggling to survive. Some saw a husband, a child, a mother sucked into the relentless current. They heard voices pleading. "There was nothing anybody could do," said eyewitnesses. It was especially hard, when the

16

voice was that of a child.

Onc father, in his attempt to escape, lost his children to the fierce waters. With his wife clasped in one arm, he clung to a wire fence with the other. But the water was stronger and swept his wife from him, leaving him only a few scars on his hands to remind him of his loss.

Another father moved his family to the attic, only to be threatened by rising water even there. He knocked a hole in the gable end of the house and passed his family out, one by one, over a two-foot cornice onto the roof, they awaited rescue.

One elderly couple attempted escape by car, but the rushing waters swept it against a tree. They waited courageously for daybreak, standing in the backseat of their waterlogged car with their noses against the top to breathe.

Gertrude Lux, 70, a small, rather frail-appearing woman, stood for five hours in almost shoulder-high water balancing her 16-year-old physically and mentally retarded granddaughter on a large foam mattress.

Another woman is haunted by the memory of her husband calling to her for help as the waters swept him away. His body was found three days later in the bottom of a grease pit in a filling station five blocks away.

People prayed. Silcntly. Openly.

People clung to whatever they could find and waited for dawn.

Rescue operations began immediately. Local firemen and law enforcement officers, 1,800 members of the National Guard in the Black Hills for summer exercise, and civilian volunteers began the search to find the living and retrieve the dead.

The rescuers snatched bodies from the water and put them on stretchers. "Just one right after another," said an eyewitness. Homeless survivors moved into aid stations, some in their nightclothes, cold and dripping. Stunned, they were unable to fathom what had happened, as they waited for news of their families.

About 150 volunteer searchers moved through the flooded area, arm-in-arm, looking for bodies. Trained dogs with handlers were brought in. A mechanical sniffer (mass spectrometer), which detects and measures gases, was flown from Washington, D.C., to help in the unpleasant task. Bodies of victims, often battered beyond recognition, were found pinned beneath trees, crushed in their gravel-packed cars or trailer homes, or buried in the debris.

Lists of names of the missing and dead were tacked on a bulletin board in neat, alphabetical order. Each day as more family members found each other, the missing list shrank from the original 4,500, and the list of identified dead grew. The final count of the dead was 234. Among them were doctors, merchants, Indians, professors, housewives, children, a priest. The prominent and the little known. Old and young. Residents and tourists. Those who had been flooded and those who had tried to help. Among those who lost their lives were firemen, National Guardsmen, and civilian volunteers.

Property damage was estimated at $75 to 100 million with only $13 million of this insured. Six thousand families were affected, 2,000 cars destroyed, and 125 businesses damaged.

Worldwide attention focused on Rapid City immediately. Offers of help and messages of goodwill poured in.

In numerous communities in South Dakota and outlying areas, the news of the disaster was picked up with more than the casual response of the average television viewer. To these men it was a signal to get out their boots, work clothes, and shovels for a few days. They were members of Mennonite Disaster Service (MDS), a grass roots volunteer organization of the Mennonite and Brethren in Christ churches in the United States and Canada.

A Mennonite Disaster Service volunteer scoops out mud left behind by Hurricane Agnes at Wilkes-Barre, Pennsylvania, in June 1972. MDSers mudded out 7,000 homes in this area in 11,000 days of free labor over a period of four months.

Like the Boy Scouts, MDS is always ready to move into action when needed. When a natural or man-made disaster strikes in any part of the United States, Canada, or sometimes in overseas countries, MDS is ready to go.

In South Dakota, Clifford Preheim, MDS coordinator for the state, heard the news of the massive flooding. In McPherson, Kansas, Marvin Hostetler, MDS coordinator for the Central States, heard it. Both men knew that national emergency relief agencies would move into action immediately. But they also knew that in addition to the American Red Cross, the Office of Emergency Preparedness, the Salvation Army, and other agencies, a disaster of Rapid City proportions always had room and need for more volunteers. In 1972 MDS had a twenty-one-year track record of thousands of volunteer days given to others in need. The motto of the organization is: "Bear ye one another's burdens, and so fulfil the law of Christ." In Rapid City, thousands of people struggled with burdens without immediate answers.

Who would go to Rapid City to direct the volunteers in this record-breaking disaster? The closest Mennonite churches to Rapid City were located at Freeman, South Dakota, but the small congregations there felt inadequate to spearhead a project the size of this one.

Marvin Hostetler, who has traveled thousands of miles as MDS project director, coordinating the activities of MDS volunteers in Kansas and other points, couldn't go because he was convalescing from a farm burn accident.

He phoned Syd Reimer, MDS chairman for Manitoba, Canada, living at Rosenort, who had been involved with MDS for about ten years, but who had no experience directing a large project. Southern Manitoba, where thousands of Mennonites live, lies about 450 miles from Rapid City as the crow flies.

"Do you know of anyone who can go to Rapid City to

direct the MDS project?" asked Hostetler.

Reimer agreed to accept responsibility for directing volunteer efforts for two or three weeks.

The flood had occurred on Saturday. Wilbur Swartzendruber, secretary-treasurer for the Central States region of MDS, from Wellman, Iowa, arrived on Sunday by private plane. Clifford Preheim arrived next. He and his wife, Dorothy, were to spend most of the summer there.

Reimer left his job as division manager of Investors Syndicate Limited and left for Rapid City on Tuesday. Nelson Hostetter, executive coordinator for MDS from Akron, Pennsylvania, came the same day. Word went out immediately to Mennonite and Brethren in Christ churches in Canada and the United States that volunteers were needed in Rapid City.

The next day, June 13, MDS set up a temporary office to coordinate volunteer activities in cleanup and rebuilding for as long as they would be needed. They projected an approximate four-week effort. Father William O'Connell offered them the facilities of the Lady of Perpetual Help Catholic School as headquarters. They accepted and moved in. The Office of Emergency Preparedness arranged initial contacts for them with other agencies and supplied equipment.

The American Red Cross agreed to supply meals above U.S.D.A. commodities as well as cots, blankets, towels, and soap for volunteers. Women of the parish, assisted by MDS volunteers, cooked the meals. The Red Cross also assumed the cost of all utilities, including electricity and gas for cooking, telephone hookup and service, laundry service, as well as inoculating all volunteers and providing first aid care. The Salvation Army supplied snacks for workers. Group insurance with a full disability plan was carried by the international MDS organization.

Recruiting for this giant-sized project was done

mostly from South Dakota, Manitoba, and Kansas. Cliff Preheim recruited volunteers from the Freeman area, helped in locating the most needy places for volunteers to work, and kept tools and equipment in working condition.

The Canadian division of MDS has no funding of its own but works under the umbrella of Mennonite Central Committee (Canada), an inter-Mennonite relief agency. It turned to this agency for support for transportation costs of volunteers from Manitoba to South Dakota.

"We had everything in our favor to make it easy for volunteers to come," said Reimer. School was out, so students could help. The offer of transportation from MCC (Canada) helped, although many others came at their own expense, some a thousand miles or more. Young people arrived by the hundreds and eventually constituted about 50 percent of the total 1,500 volunteers.

In Manitoba, the spring crops had been planted and farmers were experiencing a slack period, so they could come.

June, July, and August are vacation months for most people, so many persons and families took off one or two weeks to assist. The John Goossen family from Winkler, Manitoba, and four of their children came for a whole week.

Mennonites volunteered, but so did members of other denominations and some from no denomination.

"We accepted anyone as a volunteer who didn't look dangerous, including transients," says Reimer with a grin. Whether he was a barefoot or long-haired hippie didn't matter. If the volunteer agreed to abide by MDS personnel standards and curfews and was willing to work, he was accepted. A day spent slogging in the mud turned almost everyone into a model character.

"Send us a problem volunteer," he told the churches,

"and we will surround him with a positive witness. We will take a risk with him."

On Wednesday the first MDS volunteers began trickling in. By the weekend the first small wave of fifty to sixty was on the scene ready to work. In later weeks, the number grew to several hundred volunteers each day. Reimer, on his first field assignment as project director, felt overwhelmed at first by the size and complexity of the task before him. Where does one begin a massive volunteer operation with hundreds of eager helpers waiting for job assignments? Where does one find those who need help? Whom does one help?

During the first weeks MDS received referrals from the Red Cross for those who needed initial cleanup, but eventually developed its own system. True to its principles, it tried to assist first the elderly, infirm, handicapped, widows, people with low incomes—those who could not help themselves.

An average of 200 workers—men, women, and young people—registered per day at the temporary office for the first five weeks. Here they received their MDS buttons and car identification stickers so they could pass behind National Guard lines.

New to the area, new to helping in disaster assistance, the volunteers needed orientation. So each evening the volunteers gathered to talk about such things as boots, shovels, meals, laundry, and why they were there.

Although the most obvious task seemed to be to help in "mudding out" homes and repair work, Reimer directed the volunteers to think of the individual. "People are more important than property," he insisted. The goal of the MDS volunteers must be to restore a sense of normalcy to a chaotic situation and to help individuals regain a feeling of personal dignity in the face of overwhelming loss.

"We are here to give moral support through our presence," he told them. "Take time to listen, for what can you say to a woman who has lost husband and six children?" The leaflet MDSers offered to victims said it best, "We may be strangers to you but you are our neighbors. We cannot understand your loss, but we want to share your burden." (See Appendix E.)

Each volunteer who stood before Reimer's desk needed a job. Each job often needed a crew foreman. "They were all strangers to me," said Reimer. "I chose job foremen by look and attitude and speech."

As each new day of work began, he was sometimes left with only a few veterans from the day before and two hundred new people. "One of the persons who prays the most is the MDS project director," said Reimer.

Volunteers slept in classrooms, the gym, and spare corners of the Catholic school. Only those who knew that the Mennonite Church had originated with a disgruntled priest named Menno Simons, who left the Roman Catholic Church during the Reformation, found this situation ironic.

The work of cleaning and rebuilding progressed as the summer wore on. Reimer, an outgoing man with a friendly personality and much stamina, had planned to be away from home for about two weeks. His stay was extended week by week. At brief intervals he returned to Manitoba to tend to his business and then came back. Persistently he and his assistants kept men and women at the job of mucking out, washing down, and shoring up homes that looked hopeless.

They faced the daily frustrations of people who come to a volunteer effort with as many kinds of motivations as there are colors of houses on flooded streets. Some craved excitement and adventure. Others sought to help—but wanted to choose whom they helped. Some saw volunteer work as a chance to get away from the home routine for a while. Others thoroughly enjoyed the challenge of muscle-straining work and seeing order restored from chaos.

Mark Bruce, John Bruce, and Chester Stromsky — part of
a traveling church group who stopped at Rapid City,
South Dakota, to help following the flood in 1972. They
offered their services for a day to work alongside other
MDSers in the cleanup along Rapid Creek.

Yet sometimes even the purest of motivations—the desire to be a caring person whose motivation is the love of Christ—became dingy when smeared afresh each day with smelly, sticky mud. Some didn't like the food. Others complained about Rapid City's hot summer heat. Some were rambunctious. Some volunteers wanted to be Good Samaritans without getting mud on their jeans. Some just didn't know how to get a handle on the job, said Reimer.

Some volunteers couldn't see why they were expected to help any and all people. One group reported the woman they had been sent to help was a prostitute "with a bunch of men sitting around drinking." Nothing doing, they weren't going to help those who could help themselves. But with a little encouragement, they went back and helped them.

Sometimes when volunteers went to homes to offer their help, they faced hostility. The flood victim didn't always appreciate help from a pacifist group.

But by and large, the volunteers were a hardworking bunch of people who cheerfully tackled any job. Though too much work and too little sleep pushed everyone to the limit, each imperfection in the operation only made clearer to all concerned the importance of person-to-person programs of caring. The frustrations were offset by the wholehearted thanks and appreciation MDS volunteers received from their many new friends. "The name 'Mennonite' was holy in Rapid City," said one volunteer unbelievingly.

After a long day on the job, the entire group assembled in the evening to talk about it again. They sang and shared the experiences of the day. They prayed together. "MDS volunteers in Rapid City represented a lot of prayer power," said Reimer. Congregations at home prayed for their members, and parents prayed. "My son became a Christian at Rapid City," one parent told Reimer.

The testimonies of volunteers who had arrived earlier inspired newcomers for the work they would be doing the next day. They heard stories of the widow who had seen her husband swept away in the first huge wave after the two had finally decided to heed the flood warnings.

They heard of the ambitious young man who was stuck with a ninety percent mortgage on a $130,000 first-year motel ruined by water. The salvage help provided by MDSers gave him courage to rebuild rather than file for bankruptcy.

They heard of the military man who had come home from Vietnam because his house had been flooded. He was upset because no one was helping him. One afternoon a busload of fifty young people and some parents arrived at the MDS desk.

"Take the afternoon to look around and then we'll get you started tomorrow morning," advised Reimer.

"No," they said. "We want to start working at once."

Reimer sent the whole group to the home of the military man. By evening they had finished the job.

"What do I owe you people?" the man asked later.

"Nothing," was the response. "We want to show our faith in Jesus Christ." The man broke down and cried.

The major MDS operation in Rapid City was mud cleanup, scrubdown, and restoration of buildings. MDSers wiggled into crawl spaces, emptied heating ducts filled with mud, pumped out basements, winched heavy furniture out of houses and salvaged it with MDS and Office of Emergency Preparedness trucks for families whose homes were marked for demolition. A group of Mennonite engineers in Denver assembled special conveyers and shipped them to Rapid City, to make mud disposal easier.

Red Cross and MDS volunteers also scrubbed down and disinfected three funeral homes and morgues after their heavy use. They rebuilt the interior of Mother Butler Center gym and the basement of Madonna Hall.

27

The men did the carpentry work and the women the finish work and cleanup.

On June 28 the National Guard took a group of officials, including Reimer and other MDS leaders, on a flight of flooded areas. They viewed the heartbreaking sight of washed-out bridges, flooded farmlands, and houses scattered about like matchsticks.

Thursday of the same week Herman Regier, another MDS official, and Reimer scouted the Keystone area, about twenty-two miles from Rapid City. The next morning a busload and four carloads of volunteers went to work there. Among the families whose houses received either total or major damage there was that of Tom and Marie McKiernan, who owned a curio shop.

"The flood hit us like two by fours," Marie said, "and then the raindrops came down in torrents so that you could not see three feet away. Soon we had water rushing into our home and business. Where there had been twelve supports in our basement, there were in no time only three. We were helpless, despairing."

Noah Hege, one of the assistant MDS directors, and his volunteers found the discouraged McKiernans. Hege operated a large corn and dairy farm in Wisconsin. An early visit to the Rapid City disaster scene filled him with deep concern for the stricken people. When he was forced to return home for the haying season, he promised the Lord that if he could finish in a week, he would return to Rapid City again. With the help of his family, this became possible, and Father Noah, as he was affectionately called, returned.

He and his men found the McKiernans "at the end of our rope," as Marie put it. "They tied a knot in the end of it, and we were able to hang on. All they did was roll up their sleeves and give us their hearts."

The young people carefully washed and dried the souvenirs and placed them in plastic bags. They helped in cleanup. They offered their friendship and their faith.

At the end of the summer, the McKiernans gave Syd and Helen Reimer two candles. One had been used the night of the flood. A note attached said, "This candle was used during the flood. It is given in memory of the spiritual darkness we have lived in. You Mennonites have lifted us out of this darkness. That was your greatest gift. May God be with you always."

On July 15, MDS moved to the Presbyterian campsite at Thunderhead Falls, a beautiful hideaway in a narrow canyon along Rapid Creek supplied with individual cabins, a kitchen, dining hall, and chapel. This campsite had suffered flood damage, so the summer program had been canceled. MDS volunteers repaired the damage, mainly to the dining hall, and then used it for the rest of the summer.

As the Red Cross phased out its operations, responsibility for cleanup and repairs was turned over to MDS. Earl Boyts arrived on July 15 from Harper, Kansas, to direct the MDS carpentry work. Marie, his wife, became the official head cook and the unofficial "Mom" of all youthful volunteers.

About the middle of September, MDS began to phase out its cleanup operations and to plan for the next stage in its program of helping disaster victims in Rapid City.

It was also time to start tallying figures and adding accounts. Thanks in the form of letters and donations rolled in. Tom and Marie McKiernan traveled all the way to the annual MDS All-Unit Meeting at Altona, Manitoba, in February 1974 to express their thanks and the thanks of the Rapid City people to the delegates and friends gathered there.

"I was raised in a Christian home and had been a Boy Scout," Tom said. "Later I was wrapped up in my Air Force career and in making money. Then on that fateful day, Noah Hege and his men came to us. Since then some of you have returned and held church services. You built our belief. You gave me faith in God."

Father Bill O'Connell, who attended the annual All-Unit Meeting of MDS in Morton, Illinois, in 1973, said, "I come to thank you as a town, as a church, and as a friend—and particularly as friend. For the churches, the Mennonites were a leaven. You gave a new idea to a great many of our people as to what church people ought to be like. Your presence enabled the churches to come alive. I came to say thank you, to say that I am pleased to have such wonderful brothers and sisters in the world who just happen to be called Mennonites."

MDS found itself in the strange position of not only receiving thanks of all kinds, but of needing to say thanks to many people for what they had done for MDS. The list included the American Red Cross for its strong support with meals, bedding, supplies, and equipment; the Office of Emergency Preparedness, now The Federal Disaster Assistance Administration ("It sold us to the people," said Reimer); the Presbyterians for the use of their camp; the Church Disaster Response (CDR), an ecumenical force and fund established to meet community and individual needs, which offered MDS the first opportunity to use $33,000 of their allotted budget for rebuilding materials. "They gave us a blank check for building materials and let us write in the figures," said Reimer. CDR also designated future excess funds for MDS use to make it possible for volunteers to return the following spring and summer.

MDS had enjoyed especially good relationships with the Catholics in the area, whose facilities they used so extensively. Father Bill O'Connell, the first Catholic priest many Mennonites ever called by his first name, became "Mr. Everything," said Reimer. He was a man with a big voice and bigger spirit. He liked the Mennonites and their cooking, and above all he shared their faith in Jesus Christ. He became their friend. Later he preached at the wedding of the Reimers' daughter in Manitoba. His warm, evangelical approach won the hearts of many of the conservative Mennonites.

Through this project, MDS in Canada received a clear confirmation that it needed to continue to be organized even though major disasters seem not to occur in Canada as often as they do in the United States. Canadians could help, even if they lived hundreds of miles away.

The project proved that members of many denominations can work together, and that Mennonites, with as many varieties as Heinz products, can leave differences behind when the need requires it.

The final tally, briefly summarized, was this:

Total volunteers		1,500
Canada, mainly Manitoba	309	
Kansas	321	
South Dakota	319	
Other states (24)	551	
Total volunteer days worked		7,000
Total meals served by Catholic and MDS women		35,000
Homes cleaned		600

About 25 percent of the volunteers were from the Church of God in Christ, Mennonite (Holdeman), who officially opted to join MDS in this project. Volunteers from Manitoba, who had their transportation costs paid, usually stayed twice as long as the Americans. Approximately forty percent of the work was done by them. All volunteers worked without remuneration. Costs of meals and housing were borne by other agencies and donations.

Before the Reimers and the Cliff Preheims left, they arranged for a Christian contact couple, Mr. and Mrs. Raymond Lautt of Harvey, North Dakota, to remain in Rapid City during the winter months. The Lautts continued to supervise rehabilitation efforts for flood victims and prepared for new volunteers to work the following summer. MDS would return, but in a slightly different capacity.

Throughout the summer's work, disaster victims, reporters, and officials nosed around, curious about "these Mennonites." What makes people care so much for people they don't know? What makes them leave families, jobs, and businesses to come to Rapid City to clean up and rebuild other people's houses, going home only long enough to check up on things and then returning again? How does MDS line up volunteers so quickly? How is it funded?

The remaining chapters of this book attempt to answer some of these questions.

Chapter Two

"THE MENNONITES
ARE HERE!"

The shrill ring of the telephone breaks the night silence. A man reaches sleepily for the receiver. Subconsciously he knows what the message will be. A disaster has occurred. Help is needed.

It could be almost any kind of disaster, natural or man-made:

A tornado has whipped through a community tossing about houses, furniture, cars, trees, and people like confetti, or

The cycle of vicious rains of the past few days has caused the river to surge out of its banks. A dike has collapsed. Homes are flooded, cattle stranded, and farmlands inundated, or

A hurricane has caused an avalanche of soil and water to careen down the mountain slope, taking everything in its way: houses, trees, large rocks, small bridges, automobiles, livestock, and railroads, or

A fire has swept through part of the business section of the city, or

The earth has heaved under its burdensome load, toppling buildings, crumpling highways, and splitting mountains.

Such major disasters headline daily newspapers. News of other tragedies may not reach the next town:

A father is hurt in a farm accident and cannot attend to his crops, or

The hogans in an Indian village have been damaged by rain, or

Some homes in the inner city, left unrepaired for years, are no longer fit to live in.

But the man answering the phone is no longer sleepy. His work for this day and perhaps for several days and weeks as MDS unit coordinator has begun. He must set in motion the chain of communication which will swing Mennonite Disaster Service into action. If he is absent when the call comes, his wife is usually prepared to take his place.

This first report of disaster may come to the unit coordinator by telephone, radio, television, or newspaper. The next step is almost automatic. The coordinator sends a field director with one or two assistants to the scene of the disaster to determine the kind and extent of damage that has occurred.

The unit coordinator establishes contact with the United States or Canadian government officials—depending where the disaster occurs—with the Red Cross, the National Guard, Civil Defense, state or provincial emergency and disaster recovery departments, and other organizations which are usually already at the site. MDS also cooperates with county, municipal, and local governmental agencies, community disaster assistance organizations, including Lions Clubs International and Inter-South or Interchurch disaster response programs, and the domestic disaster department of Church World Service. Some of these organizations will be familiar with MDS from previous experience. Although MDS is registered as a federal relief agency, together with the American Red Cross and the Salvation Army, it remains a volunteer service.

This advance crew determines how many volunteers are needed, the work they will do, and what equipment will be required. They survey, plan, and pray for the best kind of emergency response. They try to determine how

An airlift of Kansas MDS men to Mississippi for hurricane cleanup in 1969.

MDS can help. Their concern is to get volunteers to the scene as soon as possible—perhaps the same day.

One field director reported that as he passed a dairy farm ruined by a tornado, a dejected dairyman stood in the middle of what had been a corral, staring at his thirty milk cows, their udders heavy with milk. Every building on the farm had been damaged or demolished. He had no water, no electricity. The dairy barn had no roof.

Only one other man was present, and he was taking pictures of the dairyman and his misery. The MDS men introduced themselves, then suggested the tractor could be dug out and the vacuum line used to milk the cows. Though they could not stay to help him, they assured him volunteers would arrive soon. "The man was about three inches taller when we left," said the field director.

If the disaster is too large for a local unit to handle, the national MDS coordinator from Akron, Pennsylvania, may fly to the stricken area to coordinate services available from other regions of the United States and Canada. He acts as liaison officer for the regional organizations. When he receives calls for help from halfway across the country or around the world, whether in Haiti, Alaska, or Yugoslavia, he knows where to turn for help. He can rally Mennonites from coast to coast, some willing to spend weeks or even months away from home to assist in long-term reconstruction following a disaster.

The national coordinator then gets in touch with regional coordinators—there are five for the United States and Canada—who in turn contact state and local unit leaders. The unit leaders call the congregational contact men, who know where to find helpers and equipment.

The reception of MDS when they first arrive at the disaster location is not always easy or pleasant. National coordinator Nelson Hostetter and two assistants penetrated the almost inaccessible scene of flood disaster at Buffalo Creek, West Virginia, by helicopter, jeep, and horseback. They drained four feet of water and mud from the community center to have a dry spot to unroll their sleeping bags. Three days later 63 men from Virginia came, some of them Quakers and Koinonia Farm people.

Marvin Hostetler, McPherson, Kansas, was sent by MDS to survey the situation in Galveston, Texas, following Hurricane Inez in 1966. The Red Cross office had advised Hostetler and his assistant to go into Galveston to set up the unit, so they chartered a small plane to transport them. "Remember the airport is open only for rescue and emergency service," they were cautioned. "Watch out for logs and debris since the airport has been under three feet of water."

At the Galveston airport the pilot asked if there was any communication or transportation to the city. One man shouted, "No, there is not, and there is a curfew in the city. You'd better be off the streets by seven o'clock or you'll be shot."

Another man who sat nursing his woes with a bottle of liquor as the MDS men described their mission grunted, "I'm not a churchman. All I have ever heard in a church is preachers telling people how good they are." They explained that since faith in Christ leads to works, they were there to serve people in need. He said, "If this is what your church means to you, I am for you. Anything I have here is at your disposal." He was their friend for the three days they surveyed the region. He even wanted to buy food for them.

On other occasions, the doors are wide open to the coming of MDS volunteers.

In Wilkes-Barre, Pennsylvania, the city heaviest hit by Hurricane Agnes in 1972, volunteers mudded out 7,000 homes in 11,000 days of free labor in four months. When the 200 volunteers left Souderton, Pennsylvania, in a caravan of five busses and 35 trucks to travel the 85 miles to the disaster area, they resembled the victorious entrance of an invading army. "God be with you," shouted the disaster victims as the cleanup caravan moved through the debris-laden streets to homes marked for their help.

As one Kansas field director walked into the Red Cross headquarters at Port Lavaco, Texas, he heard a woman exclaim, "The Mennonites are here!" She had worked with him at Meeker, Oklahoma. She understood the purpose of MDS because she had seen volunteers at work.

Another Red Cross official greeted a coordinator like a long-lost friend: "MDS is here. We are putting you in complete charge of all mud-out operations. Here are 200 names of people whose basements are full of mud." MDS went to work.

Some officials are eager to have even one or two MDS volunteers appear and start work, for they act as a catalytic agent for hope in a depressed, exhausted community. Someone still cares.

After the initial survey, during which the field directors may arrange with Red Cross for board and lodging for volunteers if needed, they report back to the coordinator, usually by telephone. Already volunteers have been in touch with their congregational contact men, making themselves available for this particular disaster. When the signal comes to go, additional volunteers are called. One person phones another. Announcements are made at church meetings or over local radio stations. Like the gathering of the clan, MDS moves forward.

"Normally the response is bigger than you ask for," said a Kansas coordinator. "I never have to wonder about help. If we really need it and call up people and tell them this is what has happened, and this is what needs to be done, they respond."

Who responds?

Men, women, youth, retired and semiretired persons, and sometimes even adolescents, are all important members of the total team. Farmers, housewives, skilled craftsmen, office workers, students. All are welcome.

Every member of a congregation can be a volunteer. There is no official membership role. While the majority are members of some Mennonite church, participation is not limited to Mennonites. Others can help also. The requirement is a willingness to help someone in distress "in the name of Christ."

"MDS began as a layman's volunteer organization," says Nelson Hostetter, executive coordinator, "and we intend to keep it that way. We want MDS to remain person-oriented, one person helping another." MDS organization is simple, but with sufficient machinery to carry on its work effectively.

Those who work five days a week at regular jobs may arrange to take several days off, especially if they live in the immediate area of the disaster. Some on tight work schedules may arrange to take several days of vacation time to serve locally or in more distant disaster areas.

Moonlighting is common, especially in summer. When a disaster hits a community, people come home from work, eat a quick supper, and spend the remaining daylight hours in cleanup or other MDS activities.

A local director organizes crews to scrub floors and pick up debris. He knows where to get generators, sump pumps, winches and trucks and chain saws. One regional coordinator has about 2,000 men—plumbers, electricians, carpenters, and farmhands he can mobilize and send anywhere in the nation.

The volunteers come carrying buckets, brushes, shovels, drinking water, and any tools that might be helpful. Meals are usually provided by the Red Cross and snacks by the Salvation Army. The volunteers wear no fancy uniforms, only overalls or blue jeans. They drive farm trucks. They come from jobs, farm work, ball games, housework, and shopping trips prepared to work hard and get dirty. They receive no salary. They ask only, "Where can we help?"

Each volunteer wears a blue and white badge or carries an MDS identification card showing clasped hands and a cross and carrying the legend, "Mennonite Disaster Service." It is his or her passport behind cordoned lines.

When a disaster strikes, it draws a crowd like flies to garbage. Sightseers, looters, sidewalk superintendents come. Also helpers. The National Guard usually sets up roadblocks to screen the undesirables. When police see the MDS stickers on cars, they smile and wave them on.

MDS by tradition confines itself to three major areas of activity on the disaster front: General cleanup for all in need, temporary repairs, and long-term reconstruction of homes for widowed and fatherless people with low incomes, the elderly and handicapped, and the minorities and disadvantaged.

During the first phase of assistance, heavy equipment moves in. Chain saws are put in operation to clean away fallen houses and twisted trees. Where possible, building material, furniture, and personal possessions are salvaged rather than burned. Fields are cleared, streets opened, and livestock penned.

One volunteer described her work: "We shoveled and threw from houses furnishings, lifelong treasures, books, toys, food—all thick with sewage—contaminated with sticky, slimy gray mud. Then the mud itself was shoveled into buckets and dumped into the streets where the whole unbelievable mess was picked up by front-end loaders and hauled away."

Another volunteer went into the home of an older couple, about to retire, who had used the wife's inheritance to build a quadruplex, hoping to use the income during retirement. The flood filled the basement and covered the main floor with four inches of silt.

When the volunteers arrived, the woman said, "We are done . . . finished . . . washed up. Everything is lost." After the crew of MDS volunteers had carefully cleaned the house so that repairs could begin, she said, "Now we can start over again. Now we have hope again."

Sliding earth, howling winds, and rushing waters have a terrifying reality and equality to them. Floods, tornadoes, hurricanes are no respecters of person. Yet a flood always seems more difficult to cope with than a tornado. In a windstorm, a single blow breaks up the house and whisks it away. Little is left, sometimes nothing. But with a flooded home, the family wrestles day after day with the unyielding mud, uncertain if they will ever be able to live in their home again.

Human need in a disaster is real and desperate. The people, often in shock, sit numb and paralyzed. Some cry. Some pray. Some curse. Some are fearful that conditions may get worse. Some worry about the damaged homes. Should they remodel, rebuild, or move away? Some have little or no insurance for repairs or rebuilding. The threat of job loss is pressing. Some have difficulty accepting help and used furniture and clothing. Others feel too old to start again. Some are depressed. One man sat for two hours on his front doorstep holding a water hose. He had reached the end of his resources.

"We train our volunteers to convince a man that now is the time he needs our help. We never ask a man whether he has insurance, and we don't ask him what religion he is. We tell our volunteers to listen . . . listen to them tell their story. They need to talk about it," said one coordinator.

Cleanup is part of the initial help MDS volunteers give. The other part is listening. Putting an arm around weary shoulders. Praying silently. Praying audibly. Comforting. But always listening to people who want to talk about the unbelievable tragedies, the unbelievable

41

physical happenings, and the strange providences of the past few hours or days.

In Forrest City, Arkansas, one family of six remained unharmed on the floor when their house, including the carpet under them, was blown away. And in Athens, Alabama, a grandmother and children were fatally sucked up the chimney of their fireplace where they had taken refuge.

In Rapid City, South Dakota, the rushing waters pulled a little girl from the grip of her father's hand.

In Huntsville, Alabama, a child's ears were packed with mud, which led to a virus infection; the mother had a fingernail torn off.

In Drumright, Oklahoma, the matron of the nursing home sat outside watching bulldozers demolish what was left of the 101-bed building. Fifteen seconds was all it took.

In Louisville, Kentucky, the trees of a large part of the center city were destroyed—some stripped, some broken, some uprooted.

Near Athens, Alabama, two thirds of a Baptist church plant was torn away from the chapel where members were praying.

At another prayer meeting in a neighboring church, the worshipers took refuge under the pews, but the pastor was killed.

In Forrest City, Arkansas, several people piled into a bathtub, and only the tub and commode remained. The rest of the building was blown away.

In another place, a neighbor invited a woman to come to her house for shelter, but the woman refused because her husband had just come home from prayer meeting. The neighbor was killed.

Norman Wingert, secretary-treasurer of California MDS from Reedley, California, and veteran MCC worker, who visited several sites of disaster about one week after the storms, writes: "At all the scenes a

MDS prepares to reconstruct a church in Tuscaloosa, Alabama, following a tornado in 1975.

funeral calm blanketed the devastation. About the only sound was the crunch of the bulldozers pushing the debris together for loading and hauling away. A few victims were sieving the rubble for personal belongings—a ring, some money, a treasured family keepsake. I saw a family of four leaning against a car with backs to their crumpled home. They weren't talking, just leaning and gazing into the future."

It isn't hard to understand why disasters are opportune time for person-to-person contacts. David W. Mann, Phoenix, Arizona, at an MDS all-unit meeting in Fresno in 1966, said, "Our affluency has given us the false illusion of security, comfort, and safety—until a disaster suddenly wipes out all possessions and even some members of the family. . . . A disaster then often becomes the one great moment of truth in the lives of many people. Suddenly they find themselves alone, helpless, and beat. The security of the things of life has vanished. They stand stripped and naked of the props of life. Here then is the opportunity where we, through MDS, can bring the gospel to them, literally by the shovelful."

Each day on the job brings people together quite unfamiliar with each other and with each other's style of life, as in inner-city housing construction. Rural Mennonites and people from the inner city learn to know each other better as they work together. One observer said, "Often the barriers of prejudice and misunderstanding that have held them apart break down. MDSers get a new firsthand perspective on the real problems that seem to trap people in the inner city."

One volunteer confessed that helping was easier than showing acceptance of the person for whom he was doing the work. "I was jolted just a bit as I checked on a house rebuilding project to see the elderly widow lady, for whom the house was being built, walk up smoking a pipe."

And the Mennonites also get mixed together.

Three carloads of MDSers went to Texas to do repair work from Lancaster, Pennsylvania. They had never met before. New person-to-person bonds and understandings developed.

One man from Harrisburg, Pennsylvania, said, "We got Mennonites from every direction." And then like a Walt Whitman poem, he recited: "Amish, Beachy Amish, Black Bumper Mennonites, Brethren in Christ, the Wenger, Washington-Franklin County Mennonites. . . ."

And Mennonites get mixed with other kinds of volunteers: Red Cross, Civil Defense, church groups, local people.

"We had a busload of college students here from Harrisonburg, Virginia," Alabama coordinator Jonas Kanagy related. Forty-five came one day. Then the local town of Hazel Green matched it with their high school students. The fields were covered with building debris at a time the farmers wanted to get their crops out. Where to get help?

The first week the local people helped. When they returned to their own work, the Mennonites came, said Kanagy. After a few weeks, the Old Order Mennonites and Amish came. "It's wonderful," he exulted, "how it all alternated with local people."

A common experience of volunteers is that as they arrive, hungry, and weary, at the Red Cross canteen for the noon meal, the local people gather around to visit. Volunteers compare notes as they relax after the evening meal. Local people gather to chat with the people who "live their religion as well as preach it." Sharing together through hymns and a devotional period gives strength for the next day. Three hundred or more volunteers may sleep on cots in one building at night, as they did at Rapid City.

The experience of George Bisbort, Bally, Pennsylvania, may be typical of many MDS volunteers. Bisbort left his sawmill job for Athens, Alabama, in mid-April 1974 for initial cleanup. He helped remove the shattered second story and replace the roof on the home of an older man disabled with emphysema.

In a Sunday report to the Bally Mennonite Church, Bisbort said the MDS group of over 250 people, housed in a local armory, met every evening for singing, testimonies, and sharing. "By the end of the week, community people were coming, too," Bisbort said. "The week was an exciting experience in service and spiritual growth."

In locating projects, MDS keeps in mind a spiritual ministry as well as a material one. Deer Park, Louisiana, a community of 200 families, was chosen as a project site not only because it was inundated by Mississippi River floodwaters, but also because it had no Christian ministry, no church, not even any church buildings.

After immediate cleanup and repair tasks are completed, the long-term work begins for MDS volunteers, such as reconstruction of houses and other buildings. As MDS volunteers become more intimately involved with the community and as local people become acquainted with the MDS program, and see that one roof after another is being replaced, and as they come to know MDSers as Jerry, Ruth, and Bill, the bonds become stronger. The day MDS decides its work is finished is sometimes a painful one. The people want them to stay. But they have to go. They leave behind friends. And hope. And courage to begin again. And sometimes people who have decided to begin this new life in a clean house with faith in Jesus Christ.

One mother said after a tornado, "We aren't afraid of you Mennonites. You are here to help."

Another said, "I prayed bitterly. You are the answer to my prayers."

46

Or, "If we had been killed by the storm, we would not have been ready. But it is different now."

Robert Rice, Athens, Alabama, whose house MDSers were rebuilding while he and his wife lived in a house trailer, said, "Back when I was a boy when something happened, they'd all just fly in, you know, and get it back together. And that's just about the way with the people you brought down here."

Getting it back together. That's all MDS wants to do.

Chapter Three

"WHY DID YOU COME?"

A young man sloshing in the mud and muck of a Corning, New York, basement commented wryly, "We decided today that if we were working for money we would quit."

Despite the hard work, loss of income, much travel, and the pressure of their own responsibilities, MDS volunteers opt in favor of helping their fellowmen. Many of those who have served once under MDS want to do it again.

Why?

What motivation induces a limited church constituency to invest as many as 56,000 days of free labor in a single year in tasks usually difficult and sometimes quite unpleasant?

Why do they come?

A miner's widow asked Coordinator Jonas Kanagy this question in Buffalo Creek, West Virginia.

Tom and Marie McKiernan, whose gift shop was destroyed in Keystone, South Dakota, repeated it.

A group from Lancaster, Pennsylvania, who traveled to Etowah, Tennessee, reported that rooftop discussions with local residents focused on the question, "Why are you here?"

The accent was different but the question the same in Wilkes-Barre, Pennsylvania, and Corning, New York; in Haiti, and in Texas and Alaska.

48

Who pays you? Why did you come?

At a time when strikes for higher wages and negotiations for increased benefits to workers are the order of the day, the phenomenon of persons working without pay doesn't make sense. Nobody gives his time for nothing.

One coordinator asked the president of United Fruit Steamship Company in New Orleans to carry men and tools to British Honduras, where a hurricane had caused much damage. He told him about the MDS project. The president replied, "You mean to tell me this quality of men will work without pay? We would be happy to get a decent day of work for full pay."

Why do MDSers come?

The answer to this question varies with the volunteer. Some are drawn because they know that an MDS project is one place where a one-talent Christian can serve as effectively as the five-talent person. Here anyone can shine, even when covered with mud.

Some volunteers come to satisfy their wanderlust. They can see the world, almost for free, in exchange for work, which they give gladly. Some are curious to see the havoc created when a hurricane or tornado sweeps through a community. Some come out of a genuine desire to help. They enjoy the good, clean feeling of working hard at a difficult task in which all the benefits accrue to their fellowman.

One volunteer who had left his farm work with his older children brought a carload of workers to Rapid City for the second time. He said, "You just can't go home and turn your back on these people in need."

Some come to pay a debt of gratitude for God's gracious dealing with them in the past. One Canadian volunteer had seen much tragedy in his lifetime. He fled Russia with the German army in 1943 and escaped being killed in Dresden, Germany, only because the train that was to take them into the city center was too full.

Later he settled in Paraguay, but here again he was caught in a civil war. Eventually he resettled in Winnipeg, where the family enjoyed peace for several decades. When the call came for skilled carpenters to work at Rapid City, he took a two-week vacation at the height of the construction season to repay the debt he felt he owed to God and humanity for the help his family had received in earlier years.

Some MDSers followed the teachings of the Mennonite Church regarding involvement in the military and stayed home from the war with an agricultural deferment. Afterward, they began looking for ways to help others. With the organization of MDS, they joined in its ranks as workers, coordinators, and inspirers of others. Such persons see MDS as an opportunity to show what it means to be a peacemaker in a world of growing violence.

Volunteers come with other motivations as well. Many see the potential of MDS to communicate God's love for each person. One MDS spokesman told an all-unit meeting, "Crisis situations afford excellent opportunities to act out God's love, to demonstrate that God cares. At no time are people made so aware of the fact that God loves and cares as when they are faced with a life situation that they cannot cope with alone." The volunteer's gift of his physical labor and his presence becomes a flesh-and-blood sign of God's love. Numerous reports by volunteers emphasize this aspect of their work, and stimulate other workers to donate their help.

In Oklahoma, a black woman's home was destroyed by a tornado. An MDS crew volunteered to clean up the debris and salvage what could be saved. She could not grasp the reason why the men should come so far to help her without remuneration. Finally she understood. "You are the answer to my prayers," she said.

John Jantzi from Oregon related that in Hopiland,

Arizona, the Indians had serious misgivings about the MDS project. Like typical Americans, the MDS unit started too fast on the cleanup and rebuilding after the flood. They neglected to clear all arrangements with the chief.

But slowly they won the confidence of the Hopis. One day the Indians started helping MDS volunteers in the reconstruction. Next the Hopis said, "Let us feed you for a noon meal." And they did. Afterward everyone sat around chatting.

Then the chief of the Upper Village, who had not liked white people, said, "I'd like to take a picture for the *Hopi News*. You can take pictures too." Until then MDSers had been advised: No cameras. In two minutes every man had his camera.

An experienced missionary who was present commented: "I don't believe it. Six months ago in the middle of July I could have skated right down Main Street on the ice. The feelings were that cold. Now they have been reversed."

Shortly after that, the chief offered the MDS volunteers his pickup to go to Phoenix, including gas expense.

In another state, the field director and his assistant felt led to stop at a damaged home, although they hadn't planned to. They were met by an old gray-haired couple. The man had been drinking, but was coherent enough to stress repeatedly no one could be trusted, especially in time of disaster. The men tried to win his confidence, but he brushed them off.

The next morning they visited him again. He spent the day watching MDS volunteers and talking to people they were assisting. The third day, he said, "I can't believe there are people like your volunteers, but you may work for me."

Before the day was over some of the volunteers were able to sit down on a pile of timbers with this couple and

51

explain the gospel of Christ. They prayed together, then threw their arms around each other and wept. MDSers found it hard to believe that this man and his wife were the same two persons who had met them with a gun that very morning.

Their reputation for honesty and trustworthiness has often given MDS workers a place of confidence not accorded to everyone. In one area, only MDS volunteers were allowed to work in a four-block area where a doctor's office had been demolished. People had been stealing drugs, particularly narcotics, scattered over the area. Though National Guardsmen carried rifles to protect property from looters, the MDS volunteers were trusted.

A teacher in a summer Bible school in Alabama was having a lesson on being a good neighbor. He asked the MDS coordinator if he could bring his students to the fields where volunteers were gathering up debris. "Where can we find a better example of being a good neighbor?" the teacher asked.

Although many MDS workers are willing to speak of their faith, MDS is not a case of street corner evangelism. One volunteer said, "When people are in trouble they want help, not sermons. God doesn't take a tornado by the tail and stick it in somebody's yard because they've done wrong. Disasters have always happened, and we can best show our faith by the way we react to them. That's why we help."

"We try to be very careful not to use our service as a kind of bait or come-on for conversion," said an MDS official. "We believe that our faith needs to be put into overalls. We feel that a lot of profession and little action is not good."

Another one said, "As Mennonites, we believe in faith that acts, love that reaches out a helping hand. When cows break through the fence or the neighbor's barn catches on fire, we say, 'Don't just stand there—do something!"

To overcome one's own prejudices to extend a helping hand is not always easy. After one flood, MDSers were cleaning in practically every flooded shop and store on Main Street except the liquor store. As the old couple who operated the store watched the volunteers assisting other shopkeepers up and down the street, the MDSers noticed the forelorn, forsaken attitude which bowed the old pair lower with each passing hour. Though their need was pointed out to the volunteers, some refused to work in a liquor store. Finally a pastor and three men offered to help. Yet when one of the men told his wife later what he had done, she muttered sadly, "But, Papa, Papa. . . ."

Situations such as these, which require a moral decision, force the volunteer to sort out in his mind the motivations with which he checked in at the MDS desk that morning. During the course of the day, he may confront a hundred ethical issues he will never meet in his home community:

When he sees a looter, what should he do? Should he speak to him himself or call the police or the National Guard?

Should he, a nonsmoker, agree to distribute a truck-load of cigarettes donated to flood victims?

Should he yield to the temptation to take pictures of people in their misery? Just one or two snapshots of that old lady crying by her doorstep wouldn't matter that much, would it?

When reporters question why he is slogging in the mud, what kind of answer should he give? Should he make it sound good, or tell the newsman he wanted a chance to see a new part of the country?

Sometimes the outpourings of praise and gratitude of the disaster victims leave the volunteer equally uncomfortable, especially when he knows his motives haven't been as unselfish as they look to others.

After he hears a Catholic priest pray an extemporaneous prayer just as evangelical as a Mennonite-uttered prayer, what should he do with his prejudices regarding Catholics?

Can he quietly accept the injustices which he sees occur after a disaster? What does he do, for example, when he finds out a local city government has used a tornado as an opportunity to rezone a former low-cost housing area into commercial property or into a high-cost residential area? He hears about families being dispossessed or those with low incomes being forced out of the neighborhood because they cannot afford the new $60,000 homes.

What does he do when he sees white, upper middle-class families receiving most of the immediate disaster relief and the poorer blacks across the tracks being neglected? Does he go back to clean up the moderately damaged wealthy home or ask to be transferred to the other section of town?

Though many persons would like to be a Good Samaritan, this role is not easy for all to move into. A natural self-centeredness may keep some from getting involved in other people's deeper needs. Sometimes the tragedy is simply too large and the destruction so devastating, the ordinary person fears to come close to it.

As the MDSer listens to story after story of desperate need, he perceives how inadequate he is for the task of comforting. In the presence of such total destruction and need, he senses a mystery and an awesomeness he cannot adequately describe other than to say, "But for the grace of God, there go I." Human help seems absurdly futile.

Added to these factors, MDSers recognize that daily familiarity with pseudo-tragedy, portrayed graphically on television, in movies, and in periodicals, dulls their sensitivity to other people's hurts and encourages loss of compassion. MDS, as an organization, becomes for them the opportunity to keep this compassion alive and provides the vehicle for the timid and the bold to give expression to their concern.

But sometimes even MDS volunteers get tired. The situation looks hopeless. It is hard to see beyond the debris of shattered buildings, broken glass, and sodden personal belongings or to try to bring hope to the despondent faces, haunted by fear of returning disaster.

For a fleeting moment the MDSer may be tempted to think how nice it would be to have someone build him a new home free of charge. At times people seem to be impressed only with his skills or with the fact that he is a member of a church which has many generous people. Some people seem to be taking advantage of free labor. A woman whose house MDSers have cleaned wants a high gloss on her furniture and woodwork, another wants the finish carpentry redone, another the rose bushes replanted and the hedges trimmed. Some want buildings repaired that have been eroded by time rather than by storm.

At such moments the MDS volunteer must be sure of the reason he came.

Every Mennonite knows that the answer to this question lies partly in what someone has termed the cultural memory of the Mennonites. Dr. Robert Kreider, former president of Bluffton College, Bluffton, Ohio, writes, "I suspect that every thinking, caring, sensitive Mennonite goes through life with a backpack of ambivalent feelings about his people and heritage—a sense of embarrassment in being a peculiar Mennonite and yet a sense of pride in being heir to a great, creative Anabaptist heritage.

"We have known embarrassment: a small, rural, quaint, irrelevant minority mistaken for the Amish and the Mormons, identified with the violent right and radical left, confused with the Fundamentalists, lumped together with crackpots, linked with prudery and legalism. It is no fun to be a member of a queer, 'backward' group in this modern, enlightened, emancipated world.

"We have known pride. Somehow it becomes known that one is a Mennonite, and the clerk in a strange place willingly cashes one's check. The halo begins to fit uncomfortably when one remembers the words, 'Beware when all men speak well of you.' "

Yet this mixture of pride and embarrassment at being a Mennonite releases the individual to act with freedom and openness to others. He is reponsible to maintain and continue the patterns of caring and concern established in the corporate past of his people.

Isaac Ratzlaff, a carpenter from Goessel, Kansas, told a *Wichita Eagle* reporter, "All our lives we've heard about the persecution of the Mennonites and how they went from one country to another until they finally settled here.

"My folks appreciated a kind word from anybody because it was something they never heard in Russia. We're so grateful for the freedom we can have here that it's become part of us to do the same for others. Because of the disasters our people have faced we can feel for other people when something happens, and we want to help. That's all there is to it. We want to help."

An ethnic memory. But that's only part of the answer to the question of MDS volunteerism.

Claudette Millar is mayor of Cambridge, Ontario, which was flooded in 1974. Mayor Millar is accustomed to administration and serves her community well. But she is also a sensitive spirit—and that spirit was almost overwhelmed by the human need and frustration she felt from those who looked to her for leadership during the crisis of the flood. She told Mennonite writer Urie A. Bender her experiences with MDS in Ontario.

"I met Mr. Bearinger—Eddie. He was the head of MDS, you know. Eddie Bearinger, Elmira, Ontario, is

MDS tornado cleanup at Clay Center, Kansas, in 1973

coordinator of MDS (Canada) and often serves as field supervisor. He said in his strong gentle voice—he's over six feet—with a quiet smile on his face, 'Don't worry.'

"You know, when he looked at me and spoke, I had the distinct impression, I was not to worry.

"It was chaos—it looked like chaos: pumps, buckets, ropes, shovels, Mennonites everywhere. But in the midst of all this chaos was Eddie, and a superb organization.

"I knew of the Mennonites . . . had heard of MDS— Mennonites going to Ohio and Elmira, New York. Of course, I thought they helped only Mennonites. Yet here they were—hundreds of them—to help us.

"The condition of our town was unbelievable. I was ready to accept assistance from anyone. I thought that just moving furniture out on the street would be a big help. I didn't realize the Mennonites would—you know—go right into basements and shovel out the crud. I could use a less delicate word.

"I must tell you a story. The owner of the New Albion Hotel is a Jew. He told me, 'You wouldn't believe the way the Mennonites worked in the synagogue—the Mennonites cleaned up our synagogue! Then they came to my hotel—a group of Old Order Mennonites—and asked if they could help. I said they could lift the carpet. They did. Then they asked if there wasn't something else. What about my basement? I told them they shouldn't go there. I couldn't stand the smell myself— the muck and sewage."

The Mayor asked, "Do you know what he said? 'They started there. Those Old Order Mennonites mucked out the whole messy basement. I had offered ten dollars an hour to get it cleaned up. No takers. They went in—the Mennonites went in—the whole bunch—cleaned it from end to end, because, they said they wanted to help me.' "

Mayor Millar said, "I used to think those conservative Mennonites just helped each other—to an extreme degree. That it was a kind of ethnic thing. But then we found . . . I guess you could say, when we found the modern Mennonites helping us just as much, I knew it was more than ethnicity. It had to have something to do with your faith.

"You know that faith was almost a silent thing. And it wasn't so much what your people did—*it was the way they did it.*"

The way they did it started a long time ago—when Jesus lived on earth and responded to the needs of men.

That tradition continued with Jesus' followers—Peter and John—who healed the lame man at the gate of the temple in the name of Christ.

The Anabaptists of the sixteenth century understood the same truth—and lived that way, caring for others in need.

Their children, the Mennonites, have never been able to escape this heritage. In Europe, in Russia, in North America—and more recently around the world—Mennonites have committed themselves again and again to the idea of caring service in Jesus' name.

This is the heart of Mennonite Disaster Service. Mucking out a basement in the name of Christ is one way of loving. And one of the gratifying results is in having other Christians coming to the MDSer to say, "Next year, we want to have a part in what you are doing."

Chapter Four

"NOT TILL I'VE
SEEN A MENNONITE!"

After one of the 1974 floods in the Eastern states, a rescue team found a woman clinging to a tree. They brought her down gently and were about to dispatch her in an ambulance to the hospital, but she resisted. "Not till I've seen a Mennonite," she said.

Curiosity about these "strange Mennonites" crops up frequently at most sites where the MDS teams work. Many reporters have found MDS makes good copy for a story. Articles have appeared in dailies, weeklies, denominational periodicals, youth and news magazines.

The *Emporia* (Kansas) *Gazette* carried an article about the 700 Mennonite volunteers who converged on the city from the wheatlands of central Kansas to clean up after a tornado on June 8, 1974.

Newsweek reporter William Schmidt saw the story and became curious. He interviewed MDS leaders and workers in the Kansas area, as well as national coordinator Nelson Hostetter in Akron, Pennsylvania, and wrote an article for the religion page of *Newsweek* (October 1974).

The sponsors of the syndicated television program *To Tell the Truth* saw the *Newsweek* account of MDS and became curious. They invited Nelson Hostetter and two imposters (John Horoshko, a salesman from Pennsylvania, and George Ryan, an insurance investigator from New York City) to stump the panel of experts in guessing his identity. A nationwide audience learned about MDS.

What does a Mennonite look like? If the curious expect to see persons with strange ethnic peculiarities, pious talk, and photogenic qualities, they may be disappointed. A better question might be, Who are the volunteers who participate in MDS?

Ordinary People

MDS volunteers are usually very ordinary people. The genius of MDS is not the prominent college professor, theologian, pastor, or businessman, but the common person who has time, interest, and skills to share with others.

The main sources of workers for the hard jobs of cleanup and rebuilding are the farmers and craftsmen who can arrange to leave their own work on short notice to look after another person's need. When the Mennonites first settled in the United States and Canada, they were a rural and agrarian people. Many still are. Some who have been crowded off the land by industrialization and urban sprawl have moved into carpentry and construction, giving MDS the skilled craftsmen it needs for rebuilding projects. Most still believe in giving a hard day's work to any job they undertake. If MDS volunteers have a complaint when they are out on a project, it is to stand around waiting for something to do.

Amos Zook, Paradise, Pennsylvania, skilled carpenter, father of 12, told a *National Observer* reporter that MDS was his favorite church project.

"I have been to Indiana, I have been to Louisiana, I have been down the Atlantic Coast," he said, to help clean up and rebuild homes, Mennonite and others as well, in the wake of tornadoes, hurricanes, and floods. If need be, he was willing to go again.

Though numerous urban MDSers also volunteer their

services, they find it harder to get away from their jobs. Frequently they contribute funds to make it possible for others to go.

Mennonites and Non-Mennonites

The composition of a group of MDSers is as varied as bolts in a hardware store. Compassion is not determined by the cut of the coat nor the length of the dress. Some MDSers come with plain clothes and beards, others with jeans, T-shirts, and long hair. Some arrive with apron dresses and head coverings, others with slacks and the latest hairstyle. Because members of the more conservative branches of the Mennonite Church attract news photographers, some newspaper reports give the impression that all Mennonites are alike in lifestyles. MDS is probably the broadest-based Mennonite cooperative agency within the Mennonite, Brethren in Christ, and Amish constituency, says Nelson Hostetter. About twenty kinds of Mennonites participate, from the conservative to the more modern.

Non-Mennonites have also joined to make a significant contribution. In Kentucky, MDS couldn't find a foreman until a Church of God member volunteered and served four weeks. A Lutheran couple worked alongside other MDSers in Texas.

A Vietnam veteran asked to help at one disaster site. "I have done a lot to be ashamed of," he said, "send me to the worst place." An MDS field director had the privilege of pinning an MDS emblem on his army tunic. The veteran couldn't have handled a medal with more respect the director said later.

German Baptists, Methodists, Presbyterians, and Baptists asked to join Mennonites in MDS operations in Xenia, Ohio. Workers first aided city officials in clearing the streets. Then they moved on to roof repair, hauling debris and personal belongings, and distributing food and clothing from Red Cross centers.

MDSers repairing public property near the Washington Monument following destructive demonstrations in Washington, D.C., in 1971.

Women

The women's liberation movement wouldn't find a solid soapbox to stand on in MDS. From its earliest years, women have been encouraged to take part. Women are needed. They are effective in washing down and mopping out flood-damaged houses after the heavier preliminary cleaning has been done. They search out stranded and isolated victims. Mennonite nurses have served through MDS, usually assigned to Red Cross teams, with whom MDS cooperates closely in emergency work. One husband and wife team worked together in carpentry construction.

Women give encouragement to disaster victims, and provide child care for them and for MDS volunteers. At Gulfport, Mississippi, when Hurricane Camille victims waited in long lines together with their children at the Red Cross center, MDS women moved up and down the lines, bringing water to the children, comforting them, and looking after other immediate needs. Some MDS women have prepared kits of toys and games to amuse children.

Women sometimes serve as long-term cooks and matrons for MDS crews and in Red Cross food canteens and in clothing distribution. The Red Cross has occasionally asked MDS to accept excess supplies left over after emergency relief has ended. These supplies are sent to the nearest MCC clothing center for shipment to other areas of need.

Women with secretarial experience look after the temporary field office, the records, and the telephone.

"We like to have a woman on the phone. We feel it encourages the disaster victim more to hear a feminine voice responding and being ready to help," says Nelson Hostetter, national coordinator.

One woman MDSer said, "I told them I couldn't do much, but I could wash dishes, which I did. When I left home, I had envisioned working with other Christian

Marjan Somer, Mennonite Central Committee trainee from Holland, was one of the many MDS women who aided in Virginia following the fury of Hurricane Camille.

women. Little did I realize that I would work in a place that had a bar. The people I worked with had many questions about my work and the Mennonites."

They asked her why she didn't drink, how many hours a day she prayed, and why she was working there for nothing. While washing dishes she was able to lead one of the girls back to faith in Christ. "When we were ready to leave, the people wanted us to stay and start a church," she said.

Youth

Kansas youth were involved in MDS work at least as early as 1952, shortly after MDS first began operations. In the years since, young people have become an increasingly larger percentage of the total number of volunteers.

Forty-two students traveled to South Sioux City, Nebraska, in 1953 to clean up the home of a 91-year-old woman whose few possessions had been soaked in the flood. One of them said, "Many of us who volunteered had often longed for the privilege of doing some specific voluntary service, and we eagerly took advantage of the call given to us."

"Young people are attracted to MDS today because it is one church program geared to be flexible and to follow contemporary needs," says national coordinator Nelson Hostetter. "It's a new program for the now generation.

"It's surprising how many young people know something about building and want to put their skills to work in a cause they can believe in," he says. "Vocational-technical schools and summer job experience have given young people a chance to acquire construction skills. Now they have an opportunity to use them."

The percentage of youth among the MDS volunteers rose most sharply in Rapid City, South Dakota, after the 1972 flood. Of the 1,500 volunteers who registered,

50 percent were under twenty-five. The number is growing in other MDS projects as well.

To accommodate this increasing involvement of young people, MDS has arranged for two special kinds of youth activities in addition to the regular cleanup work.

Youth Squads were organized for the summers of 1973, 1974, and 1975. For ten weeks high school and college students and others took time off from their regular schedules and teamed with adult leadership at various disaster sites to continue the work of cleanup and rehabilitation.*

Traveling Youth Squads of eight young people and a leadership couple have worked together for six months or longer, sometimes staying only a short while at one place, sometimes longer in flood and tornado projects.

"People complain about our youth," said one coordinator. "I met so many of the other kind of young people, I didn't have a chance to think about problem youth. If at first some of the older people may have looked sideways at the long-haired kids, by night they all looked the same—muddy."

A young volunteer gave his point of view: "Some of the young people salve their conscience by working in

---

*During the first three years of these youth programs, the following statistics were compiled:

1973: 77 participants divided into groups worked at Buffalo Creek, W.Va.; Corning-Elmira, N.Y.; Rapid City, S.D.; Wilkes-Barre, Pa.; 61 were from MCC-constituent churches, 16 from other denominations.

1974: 59 participants worked at Buffalo Creek, Corning-Elmira, and Wilkes-Barre and four new points: Athens, Ala.; Glen Allan, Miss.; Porcupine-Wounded Knee, S.D.; and St. Maries, Idaho; 52 were Mennonite and 7 non-Mennonite.

1975: 62 participants at Brandenburg, Ky.; Denver, Colo.,; Omaha, Neb.; Warren, Ark.; Xenia, Ohio; 55 were Mennonite and 7 non-Mennonite.

the disaster areas. They get ridiculed quite a lot for being draft dodgers, but that's not the reason I'm here. I don't believe I have to justify my feelings about war."

Out of this growing involvement of youth in MDS have come all kinds of stories about this new breed of youth.

At Elmira, New York, twelve to fifteen Inter-Varsity students who had attended the evangelistic meetings of Mennonite evangelist Myron Augsburger planned to volunteer. On the way to Elmira, their car broke down. A stranger they met en route gave them a fully equipped Winnebago to drive to their destination, no strings attached, after he heard what they wanted to do.

A young boy drove his old car all the way from Canada to Rapid City to help out. "He ran out of money for gas and his tires were almost worn through," says Dorothy Preheim, wife of the state MDS coordinator. "But he wouldn't take any money from me. He finally consented to taking five dollars to fill up his gas tank."

Also at Rapid City, Stan Walberg, a Hill City teacher, who has operated Wild Cat Cave since 1954, gave a discouraged call to MDS for help in mucking out his cave. He got it. Three long-haired youths.

"They were, I guess, what you might call hippies," said one of the MDS personnel. But they were willing to work in the cave. Another four young men joined the group. Then a pack burro named Maria and a mule they called Maggie May became part of the cave team. They gave each other prehistoric names like Torak and Grunk. And worked. The cave got cleaned, the young men enjoyed the challenge, and oldsters developed greater toleration for long-haired youth.

The young people have been open in sharing their feelings about the experience wherever it took place. Typical comments include:

"When I came to Rapid City, I wanted a chance to

Elaine Peters, Niverville, Manitoba, works with children in a day-care center as part of her summer 1973 Voluntary Service experience in Rapid City, South Dakota. Of the 1,500 MDSers who registered to help at Rapid City, more than half were young persons under 25.

work for Jesus, a social experience, and a good time—in that order. I got all three."

"One thing which bothered me about the people was that everyone seemed to be praising the Mennonites without realizing that they should be praising God, for if it wasn't for God, the Mennonites would not be in Rapid City. It made it just too easy to work for wrong motives."

"Wow! Mennonites have a lot going for them. This summer we've been treated like we were extra special."

"It seemed as though we were helping people who were not really desperately in need of help. If one enters a house which has a huge frig, a stove, a dishwasher, and a microwave oven in the kitchen and a fireplace and thick rug in the living room, one begins to wonder a bit. . . ."

"I've really loved this summer, and I want to thank you for letting me come out and be a part of it."

Retirees and Vacationers

Another special group becoming more involved in MDS is the golden-agers. "Retired people are a valuable asset to MDS," says Nelson Hostetter. "People are retiring earlier. They own a trailer or other means of travel and are able to support themselves, yet they don't want to travel and do nothing."

The MDS head office suggests to the traveling retired couple they donate some time to a disaster project which will fit their itinerary. The office gives them a list of projects and phone numbers to call. It also sends the field directors at the disaster sites the names of these people.

Al Kurtz, Sarasota, Florida, who owned an air conditioning, heating, and plumbing business, sold out his business and applied to MDS. "Instead of waiting for retirement, I would like to give a year now in voluntary service," he said.

Kurtz has been appointed as traveling project director and his wife, Hilda, as a food specialist. Other retired and semiretired persons with years of experience and expertise are the one-to-four-month leaders and assistant leaders on the medium and large long-term projects. Some couples arrive on location in their self-contained travel units, ready for any type of service. Some of these have picked up building and construction skills as hobbies, sometimes as a full-time occupation.

"We never sacrifice quality control because this is a voluntary agency," says Nelson Hostetter. "We use experienced persons as supervisors on the job."

Vacationing families are finding MDS a pleasant way to combine travel, pleasure, and service in one package. Some families from the East traveled to the West and spent two or three days at Omaha, Nebraska, assisting in cleanup after a tornado struck in early 1975.

And even the younger children are asking, "Isn't there something we can do?" One mother told an annual meeting of MDSers that her 12-year-old boy became one of the guides to direct crews to the right street addresses because he knew the community. She encouraged volunteers to come with families. There would be work for most age groups.

Middle-aged Volunteers

Although a good portion of present-day MDS is made up of the young and energetic and the older and retired, the large core remains the middle-aged person who grew up during the Depression, possibly spent some time in Civilian Public Service camps during World War II, and who has seen the world change rapidly around him. The leaders of the MDS movement, who come from this group, are usually men with dedication, personal charisma, and management skills learned through work experience. They have a clear vision of the "will of the Lord" for their lives.

71

John Diller, Hesston, Kansas, income tax practitioner, is widely acknowledged as the coordinator who could always be depended upon to answer the phone because he couldn't get away from it. He spends his days in a wheelchair. He represents the genius and dedication which have made MDS the nationwide organization it is today.

The day after MDS celebrated its 25th anniversary in February 1975 at Hesston, he "celebrated" his thirty-first year in a wheelchair. Thirty-one years earlier, one winter day, he helped his two young children build a doghouse. His last task of the day was to feed the cattle some silage. As he worked the winch to pull the silage from his old-style, hole-in-the-ground silo, the platform on which the winch rested slipped and he fell sixteen feet into the hole.

As he lay at the bottom of the dark silo, he thought, "Maybe this is God's way of getting me into some other kind of work." He never walked again, but was forced to leave the farm.

When the newly formed disaster organization, Mennonite Service Organization, the forerunner of MDS, asked him to become their coordinator in 1951 because he would always be available, he accepted a job which was to last twenty-one years. During this time he watched MDS grow from a small local effort to an international organization.

"They gave me a job to do and I did it. It was the Lord's work," he says simply. Like most MDS leaders, he recognizes openly the staunch support his wife, Emily, has given him. MDS has often been a husband-and-wife effort.

"In those twenty-one years he did twice as much as all the rest of us put together," is the high tribute of one of his fellow workers.

Only once did Diller visit the scene of a disaster, though he was intimately involved with all of them during his period of service. In 1955 when MDS had mustered 1,100 men to work at Udall, Kansas on Memorial Day, to clean up after a tornado, one of his MDS friends pestered him, "You've got to go to Udall and see that."

"No, I haven't got time. I've got to answer the phone," Diller insisted. He was persuaded that all available men were probably already at Udall, and his wife could answer the phone. He would be back at his desk by four o'clock.

"I saw the men at work," says the man in the wheelchair. His eyes sparkle behind the gold-rimmed glasses when he talks about MDS. "It is the only time I was at a disaster scene and. saw the men at work." The words sound wistful. Twice he coordinated MDS activities entirely from his bed while recovering from an illness.

These early leaders, such as Diller, who have watched MDS grow from a toddling infant to maturity, guard its purpose zealously. It must not become merely a cleaning outfit, intent on getting a community in shipshape condition. It must remain a group of caring people, whose goal is to give people who have been knocked flat by circumstances the courage to begin again.

Furthermore, such men see few difficulties or failures, only challenges, for how can an organization fail when it exists only to serve the volunteer and to keep the road clear so he can get to where he needs to go?

On one occasion the field director promised confidently that 100 volunteers would be ready to fly to Gulfport, Mississippi. Diller and an assistant, Dan Plett of Hillsboro, Kansas, had twenty-four hours to find the volunteers, tell them where they were going and what they needed to take along, as well as keep the National Guard informed regarding the names of the people. The long hours the two men spent on the telephone weren't resented but were seen as a job to be done.

Another time, it may have looked as if MDS

volunteers would have plenty of work for several days. The farmers would arrange for neighbors to do their chores so they could be away. But the work might wind up suddenly. Perhaps the National Guard would come with bulldozers to clean up the debris in a hurry instead of sifting through it first for what could be salvaged. But that also can hardly be considered a failure.

Such difficulties which make coordination uphill work are viewed philosophically. "It was my responsibility to help the organization do what they wanted to do," Diller says. "It wasn't my dream or my idea. The people took hold and did it. We might have done more. Some opportunities we missed. If we didn't do one thing, we did something else. We have only so many resources. During good weather it is hard to get farmers to come, for then they would have a disaster at home."

What does a Mennonite look like? The lady caught in the tree because of the flood might have a hard time recognizing one by outward appearance. Some, like Diller, aren't even around to be seen.

Chapter Five

WHEN THE
SKY FALLS DOWN

When the autumn leaf fell on Chicken Little in the story in the old grade school reader, she thought the sky was falling down. She rushed about telling her friends the terrible news.

The story amuses, yet offers a truth every MDSer is soon conscious of. Whether a disaster covers a large area, several hundred square miles in the case of a flood, or just one building, as in a residential fire, disaster is always personal. Grief is not lessened because many people and buildings are involved, nor is it less serious because only one small family is affected, and the damage seems trivial in financial terms. A disaster always feels as if the sky is falling down.

Though the big disasters reach the newspaper headlines immediately and attract helpers by the hundreds, the little tragedies—a fire in the attic, an accident on the highway, or the lengthy sickness of the wage-earner in the family—are not bypassed by MDS. These little projects easily get lost in the records, yet they are as meaningful to helpers and helped as the wide-scale disasters. Caring is difficult to mass produce like soap or shoes. It is most effective on a person-to-person basis.

How does MDS get involved in a disaster? Who decides when MDS will send helpers to persons in need? The decision to become involved in the large disasters in an immediate area is almost automatic. Yet participation in each project is determined by the local MDS unit, which functions autonomously. If the disaster is small and localized, it may be taken care of by local churches without involving MDS. Yet this does not mean that MDS disregards such small projects. They are as important as the big ones.

In the summer of 1972, a fire burned out a dry goods store in Minneola, Kansas. Persons from the Meade churches cleaned the store for the owner, who gave them the damaged clothes and yard goods. The women washed and dried what was salvageable and forwarded four truckloads to MCC clothing centers.

The storeowner said, "This group is important to our country. Many of us thought such consideration was lost. You lessened our burden and made it easier to bear."

In another place, a group of four volunteers repaired a fire-damaged parsonage chapel. Another group helped a minister to build a workshop. The list is endless. In every state and province the little stories of MDS helping others—a neighbor or the individual at the other end of the community—can be related.

This "little stuff" often omitted in the big reports includes stories of the MDSers praying for one another. To be a member of MDS is to become part of a prayer band reaching across the nation ready to lend its spiritual strength as word about a concern spreads.

On one occasion, MDS had the opportunity to help with prayer, financial resources, and physical work in an unprecedented way when Kenneth Hanson, a McPherson, Kansas, farmer, was seriously injured. This time no one debated whether MDS should help. The injuries occurred while Hanson was helping in an MDS project on a neighbor's farm.

Lying on a water bed in the hospital, paralyzed from the waist down, Kenneth Hanson watched the evening

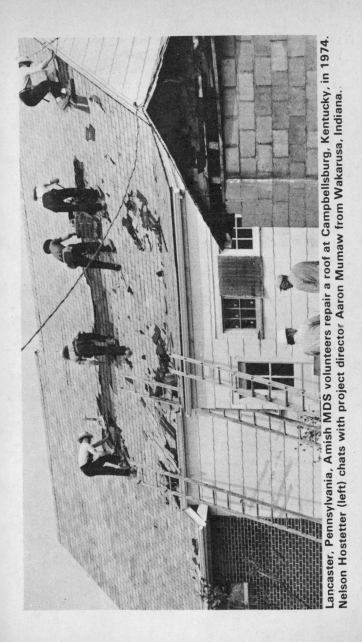

Lancaster, Pennsylvania, Amish MDS volunteers repair a roof at Campbellsburg, Kentucky, in 1974. Nelson Hostetter (left) chats with project director Aaron Mumaw from Wakarusa, Indiana.

six o'clock news. As the newscaster droned on, Hanson caught the name of a familiar city, his home community of McPherson. Across the screen rolled a fleet of tractors pulling plows, which left sharp, careful furrows behind them.

One tractor in particular caught his attention. He thought he saw his 14-year-old son, Craig, his face smudged with dirt, beaming at the camera as he rode into view.

Later that evening Ken watched the newscast again to verify what he thought he had seen. Yes, the boy was his son. He was riding their tractor. The land being plowed was his own. More than forty friends, neighbors, and acquaintances had gathered on his farm to clear 240 acres of wheat stubble because he couldn't do it. Young Craig was one of the group.

"It brought tears to my eyes," says Ken, "to see my boy driving out to me on the screen while I was lying helpless in the hospital."

Ken faced a long struggle to walk again following his accident while helping a Mennonite Disaster Service unit clean up a neighbor's farm following a tornado. His back had been broken and the doctors said he would never walk again. The plowing bee was only one of many kinds of mutual support given him and his wife, Grace, and their children Craig, then 14, and Tamara, 12, following the tragedy. It was the first serious accident to a volunteer in twenty years of MDS operations.

On June 14, 1971, Ken had gone to the Ralph Hostetler farm near McPherson in response to an MDS appeal for help to clean up the wreckage of barns blown down by the twister. The previous evening a severe wind and rainstorm had swept through the area doing considerable damage. On this farm all buildings except the house had been demolished. MDS had moved into action at once.

"I am not the kind of person who takes chances,"

says Ken. He was glad to offer his services to the MDS unit. "I had no indication what might happen."

About 70 to 80 men gathered at the Hostetler farm early that morning. One of their first jobs was to empty the large loft of the wrecked barn. About 10:00 a.m., without warning, the structure collapsed when it lost its support as the bales were removed. Several men narrowly escaped. Ken was caught under part of the roof.

"I saw it coming," says Ken. "The noise rumbled in my eardrums. I could hear a lot of bones break, yet I was conscious throughout. I couldn't feel a thing. I knew at once I was paralyzed."

Pinned under the roof, he watched the legs of the men as they moved hurriedly about. Marvin J. Hostetler, MDS area coordinator, had temporarily gone to a neighboring farm which had also been damaged to see if some of the volunteers working at the Ralph Hostetler farm should be transferred there. Fortunately this shift of workers had not yet taken place, for without them the collapsed roof section could not have been lifted off Ken so quickly.

At McPherson Hospital, where the first X-rays were taken, Ken and Grace, who had been contacted immediately, received the disheartening news, "You'll never walk again." Ken's back was broken, the first and second lumbar vertebrae crushed. The lower limbs and abdominal organs were paralyzed.

Because of the seriousness of his injury, Ken was immediately transferred to St. Francis Hospital in Wichita, about 50 miles away. The doctors there concurred with the earlier diagnosis. Ken would never again sit behind the wheel of a truck. He would never again sense the surge of power as a big tractor roars into action. His farming days were over. He faced the life of an invalid, or, at best, the possibility of awkward movement with the help of leg braces.

The medical team which examined him decided

against surgery, for they thought little would be gained by an operation. They foresaw a hospitalization of at least three months for Ken before he could be released as an invalid for further convalesence at home. They promised nothing.

"Yet I was never despondent," says Ken in his quiet, reserved way. I'm fearful like anyone else. Also, I'm not the kind of a person to doubt the word of the specialists, yet I was not accepting their word."

The second week in the hospital he told his wife, "I'm going to walk out of here. I'm going to play with the children again."

The news of the serious injury to one who had been helping in another's disaster quickly spread through the area newspapers as well as the Mennonite press. The calls came pouring in: "What can we do for you?"

"Pray for us," said Grace, who recognized that their immediate greatest need was not money, but spiritual strength for the struggle which lay ahead.

And people prayed. In the First Mennonite Church of McPherson, where the Hansons are members, the first few Sundays the congregation had a quiet prayer time for Ken and his family. Their need became the prayer concern of families, Sunday school classes, and individuals. From far and wide came cards and letters indicating prayer support. Some of the writers knew the Hansons; others didn't. As the men had earlier joined hands to lift the roof off Ken's back, now others were joining hands in prayer to meet another need.

To Ken and Grace the outlook continued to look bleak as far as farming was concerned. They were surely and swiftly being mustered out of it. Their immediate reaction was, "Let's get rid of the land." Yet friends encouraged them to hang on for a while.

Grace, a slight, attractive brunette, overtook the demanding job of managing the farm, which included looking after the irrigation wells. In addition, she made regular visits to her husband in the hospital and looked after the home and children. Relatives, friends, neighbors, and acquaintances pitched in to help with other tasks.

When the wheat needed to be harvested, Homer Krehbiel, McPherson, together with Marvin Hostetler, MDS coordinator, organized a combine bee. Later, another group took care of the plowing. Still others planted the row crops. On days when the men worked in the fields, the women cooked meals. Hands joined hands to make the burden lighter. "Hardly a person in the neighborhood was not involved," says Grace.

The Hansons carried only a small health insurance policy. It soon became clear that if Ken's hospitalization continued indefinitely, medical expenses would become a major burden. Those closely associated with the accident were concerned how this could be remedied.

One solution suggested immediately was to organize a Mennonite Mutual Aid Association (MMAA) group in the McPherson congregation. This churchwide health insurance plan provides that if 50 percent of the congregation enrolls, a chronically ill person such as Ken is eligible for assistance without a waiting period. However, this plan hardly seemed feasible, for MMAA was not well known in the area and a number of the congregation already were insured by their employers or carried other insurance.

A few persons gathered to discuss the matter. To enroll 50 percent in an MMAA group plan seemed out of the question. However, congregational meetings and individual contacts showed the people that MMAA was not "just another insurance company" out to get the workingman's dollar, but a clear way to share burdens and express love. A group was formed in the McPherson church.

Beginning on August 7 MMAA began to carry a share of Ken's expense. But there was still the expense contracted before the new group was formed. Another group joined hands to help with this need.

Ken learned about it the day a friend walked into his room with the words, "You don't have to worry about the hospital bill. MDS is going to take over what Mutual Aid can't pay."

"But that's charity!" Grace remonstrated later to Marvin Hostetler, MDS coordinator at the time. She, together with Ken, was determined not to make their tragedy a burden to others.

"No," clarified Hostetler, "this is not charity. This is love. This is the church. This is Christianity."

"Of all the projects we have done as MDS, this one had the biggest involvement," says Hostetler. MDS moved into action to assist in this disaster in the same wholehearted way it has helped in other types of need.

The response was overwhelming. More than $6,800 was donated of which $368 came from outside the state. National MDS was on standby and would have put on a fund drive if needed. In addition to the continuing help of MMAA and MDS, financial aid also came from the Mennonite Medical Association.

Meanwhile, Ken maintained his optimistic outlook in the hospital. On one subject he was absolutely unchanging. He refused to abandon belief he would walk again.

Visitors came by the dozen to cheer Ken up and left cheered by him. "He had a tremendous spirit," says a friend. "Jesus Christ was present with him." One day a stranger walked into Ken's room with the words, "The person with that kind of attitude I have to see . . . . "

Forty-six days after the accident on that June morning, like Elijah who was confident of rain when he saw a small cloud (like a man's hand) in the sky, Ken had the first small indication that he might walk again—he wiggled a toe. That little wiggle excited a whole community. People who had never heard of Kenneth Hanson before knew he had wiggled a toe.

But the doctors were not so optimistic. They had Ken measured for leg braces to provide him with some mobility when he left the hospital. The order was sent and the doctor in charge left for vacation.

During the doctor's absence, Ken asked to be taken to the physical therapy ward to see what he would face when he was ready for that step. While there he requested the nurses to place him in an upright position between the parallel bars.

"The first time I got up I could make my feet move," Ken remembers. The moment was exciting. When his doctor returned, he mentioned that the braces would be ready soon and Ken could begin his therapy.

"I don't think I'll need any braces," Ken maintained stoutly. The doctor persisted. "Examine me," requested Ken and showed him the slight movement in his legs.

"The good Lord has been with you!" responded the doctor. The order for braces was canceled.

Ken continued his therapy, first on the parallel bars, then with two crutches, later with one, then without any. Seventy-six days after he had been admitted—about two weeks before the doctors had suggested he might return home as a paralytic—Grace took Ken home in a friend's station wagon. He was walking—stiffly, awkwardly, with some pain—but he was walking.

Today Kenneth Hanson continues farming in rural McPherson. He can ride a truck and handle a tractor. Although he can't do heavy lifting nor walk too much at one time, he can do more than watch from a wheelchair when Tamara rides her horse. Ken is a farmer again. And he is grateful for the assistance relatives, friends, and others gave personally and through Mennonite Disaster Service, Mennonite Mutual Aid Association, and other agencies.

Although the Hanson accident was unique in the way it happened, the help MDS gave was the kind it tries to give to all individuals who find the sky falling down.

Chapter Six

A
MENNONITE DISASTER

Mennonites are no strangers to disaster in their 450 years of pilgrimage from Europe to America, to Prussia and Russia, and in more recent years, to South America and Central America.

Disaster has come to Mennonites in many forms: religious persecution, famine, sickness, the aftermath of war and revolution, drought, prairie fire, wind, hail, and flood. Like their neighbors, they have had to endure suffering time after time. Yet throughout their history, one can find stories of caring, prompted by love for Christ, which in modern times set the pattern for MDS.

One major disaster in which Mennonites who had settled in America were able to reach across the ocean to fellow Mennonites who had migrated in the opposite direction to the Ukraine, Russia, occurred a brief fifty years ago. This gesture of love became the forerunner of Mennonite Central Committee (MCC) an inter-Mennonite relief agency which today ministers to needy people in many countries regardless of race or creed. Mennonite Central Committee is the agency under which MDS operates.

German-speaking Mennonites had settled in the peaceful villages of the Ukraine about 1786 upon the invitation of Catherine the Great, who had promised them religious freedom. Until World War I, the Mennonites in this area enjoyed prosperity, good schools, full churches, and productive farms.

One writer of the times describes these happy days as a time when the streets were filled with all kinds of vehicles—heavy livery droshkies wagons drawn by shiny, well-fed horses, *droshkies* loaded with happy and healthy-looking individuals, rubber-tired carriages driven by proud landowners, and a few cars which roared through the villages, frightening children, chickens, and geese, and causing the dogs to set up a dreadful barking.

But the war changed some of that. Taxes increased. Horses, the farmer's pride, were conscripted for the army. Young men were taken from the villages to serve as medics in the army. Their religious convictions forbade them taking up arms. Yet despite these inconveniences, the war was a battle being fought on a distant front, and the Mennonite villages remained peaceful.

But the general hatred of the nation's people toward their enemy, Germany, could not be kept out of the Mennonite villages indefinitely. Gradually it was directed toward this peace-loving group of German-speaking citizens, even though they had been Russian citizens since the middle of the eighteenth century. First, Mennonites were forbidden to speak German in church services. Next came the land liquidation law, which was even more difficult for these settlers to accept, for they took great pride in their exemplary farms.

With the overthrow of the czarist government by the Bolsheviks in 1917, the revolution burst upon the entire nation. Total anarchy reigned for a while. All laws were rescinded, prisoners were set free, and the golden age of freedom became a travesty, as thieves and robbers, singly and in groups, moved through communities demanding money, gold, silver, and always horses.

Meanwhile the front of the Red and White armies in the revolutionary war shifted back and forth through the Ukraine, site of the Mennonite villages. Cannons boomed in their backyards, while the villagers waited fearfully in cellars for the day's shooting to end.

Fear and anxiety took on a new face when a large number of bandits, led by Nestor Makhno, began plundering, raping, and murdering in the fall of 1919. They stole horses—always the best ones. They confiscated wagons, furs, blankets, shoes, food. They murdered at whim. Victims in one Mennonite district totaled 245. Women and girls were raped en masse with a resulting plague of venereal disease.

But like the plagues of Egypt, the end of one siege only meant the beginning of another. After the period of brutal harassment by the Makhnovists, a new enemy moved in. Like an uninvited phantom which slips through closed doors and windows without sound, hunger stepped into their midst and stayed.

In the spring of 1921, the last of the grain in some of the Mennonite settlements was used up. Bread prices and taxes rose. New taxes were introduced almost daily, perhaps for each window in the house, for each tree in the orchard, or for each son or daughter. Eventually about fifty kinds of taxes were being enforced, and family finances were depleted. Without money, the people could not buy bread, nor was there much bread to buy. The people faced a foe they didn't know how to fight.

The large empty lofts and cellars, symbols of past prosperity and glory, taunted them. The doors of bare cupboards and closets slammed shut with a hollow ring.

Yet the villagers had hope. They planted their crops in the spring of 1921, ploughing with teams of broken-down horses and cows, sometimes only cows. Haggard men and animals were forced to rest often. Sometimes one horse collapsed while its companion stood alongside, trembling with exhaustion. Neighbors were called to pull the beast to its feet, so the stumbling around the field could continue. It was not unusual for a man and wife to harness themselves to the implements in a desperate effort to get the seed into the ground.

The work, however, was in vain. In the fall of 1921, the drought-burdened fields were barren, and the Mennonites faced winter with less food than the year before.

The famine drove some families to eat cats, dogs, horses, mice, crows, dead livestock, and even to boil leather. Bread was baked with anything that might yield some nourishment—roots, leaves, hay, corncobs, bones, weeds, bark and sawdust.

Children and adults, who had grown up with plenty, became beggars. They dragged themselves from house to house and window to window all day, crying, "Bread, if only a crumb, we are starving." Pale-faced children with sunken cheeks and eyes tried all kinds of methods to persuade adults to give them a morsel to eat. At best, most mothers could hand them only a warm cup of weak *Prips* (a substitute cereal coffee) and a bowl of clear soup.

One mother and father were sitting in their kitchen one evening pondering what the New Year would bring. Would someone help? As the mother moved about the kitchen with slow, deliberate steps, preparing the meager evening meal, she heard a sound.

Was it someone crying? No, it sounded more like singing. Yet who could sing at such a time? At first the song was soft and subdued. Then it became louder, until it rose above the howling of the winter wind.

The singer was Lena, a neighbor's ten-year-old daughter, trudging from door to door singing for a bit of bread or a few spoonfuls of soup. So young and already so burdened by life, thought the mother. Yet how could it be otherwise, when even the strongest men of the village had been weakened by the famine, both physically and spiritually.

The mother opened the door and drew the half-starved child inside. After placing little Lena by the warm stove, she gave her a bowl of soup and a tiny piece of bread. Overcome with joy, Lena responded gratefully and ate her food. Then clutching her threadbare blanket around her, she moved back into the cold.

A schoolteacher in an orphanage writes how during the worst of the famine the daily ration for the children was one pound of bread, two bowls of thin soup, and tea.

At Christmas, the season the children usually awaited so eagerly, they received no extra goodies. With glazed eyes and expressionless voices they sang the carols, then went to bed. At night she could hear them sobbing, "I'm so hungry; I'm so hungry." Yet she could not comfort them that the day of Christ's birth would bring food. Before the famine ended, forty of the children had died.

What does real hunger feel like?

Gerhard P. Schroeder,* one who experienced it, writes: "In the evening you go to bed hungry. It takes a long time to fall asleep because of the gnawing thoughts of hunger, of helplessness, of being destitute. You are perishing . . . you are going down . . . you have to die . . . slowly. You are getting weaker and weaker. . . . These thoughts drive you almost to insanity.

"In the morning you awaken with the same thoughts. You are hungry and you know your family is hungry. What will you do? You answer your own question. There is nothing, nothing, nothing you can do.

"You walk from one room to the other; you walk through your kitchen and you remember what an abundance of food there used to be in this house. The possibility of want, of suffering from hunger never entered

---

Miracles of Grace and Judgment, published by the author, P.O. Box 134, Lodi, Calif. 95240, tells of personal contacts and experiences with the notorious Makhnovshchina during the civil war in the Ukraine, 1914-23. I am also indebted in this chapter to D. M. Hofer, *Die Hungersnot in Russland und Unsere Reise um die Welt* (Chicago, Ill.: K.M.B. Publishing House, 1924).

your mind. . . . But now it is here. You are hungry."

He and his wife discouraged each other from talking about food, yet when they met a friend, invariably after the greeting the first question was, "Have you eaten today?" Everywhere one saw hungry people crying, "Bread, bread, will we get bread?"

One family had spent countless hours singing around the old organ before the famine. In times of joy, they sang of the Great Creator. In times of sorrow, they sang until the last tears had been wiped away.

As the famine prolonged its stay, one by one all furniture but the organ was sold. The father tried to convince himself the organ was an integral and necessary part of their survival. Yet one day when his small daughter questioned, "Daddy, why don't you buy some bread?" he knew it had to go also. From then on, the house was silent.

The aged, sick, and children were affected most by the lack of food. In desperation, the Mennonites turned to any source for food, wandering in the forest looking for roots and foods they would have disdained to eat a few months ago. Some landlords set up kitchens for a while for their workers, but by January of 1922 this practice was discontinued. One day the church bell slowly tolled its message of death. And then the tolling became a regular affair, and a burden to listen to.

Each week the dead had to be disposed of in ground rock-hard with frost. Men weakened by long months of hunger struggled to dig graves. One family whose child had died found the task impossible. They placed the body in a shallow hole in the ground, curled its limbs slightly, covered it with earth, sang a song, and left.

One villager tells of watching the funeral of a husband and wife. The bodies were laid out on bare boards wrapped in sheets, which made them look like mummies. The thin, bony, blackened faces of the dead peered out accusingly at the living, as if to say, "If you had shared your last bit of bread with us, would we have died?"

The congregation, raggedly dressed, sat stooped and silent. Some of the women huddled under blankets instead of traditional shawls. The preacher spoke of a wonderful place in eternity where heat and cold, hunger and thirst would be unknown. Few joined in the singing of the final hymn.

The bodies were placed on a simple wooden wagon and pulled along the rutty road to the graveyard, almost sliding off with each lurch of the wagon. The vehicle stopped before a shallow grave, and the boards with their burden were lowered into it. Beside the grave, another one was already being dug. The men took turns filling the grave because of their limited strength.

After the grave had been filled, the crowd dispersed, still silent. No one had words at such a time. In a few weeks, three sons of the same family were buried there also.

In the face of such intense suffering, hearts became like stone. Some people could no longer cry, as they watched member after member of their family slowly succumb. One mother whose children were too weak to walk could only give them salt water when they cried to her, "If only I had a piece of bread, I would get well."

Attempts were made to maintain school, but the children no longer learned anything. Like wilted flowers they sat in their benches, dull, disinterested. Services were held in the church when possible. Each Sunday the minister read the death list and cause of death—usually starvation or typhus fever. As the monotonous words fell on their unlistening ears, no one showed visible signs of mourning but sat pale and dumb in their misery.

Hunger stalked the Mennonite villages and surrounding communities that winter—children and adults, men and women, Mennonites and Russians. Only those who have faced such total tragedy know how difficult it is to

keep alive faith in a sovereign, just, and loving God—
unless someone reaches out a hand filled with love and
hope.

Each day of extended suffering, the victim assures and
reassures himself that nothing can separate one from the
love of God, that God is still alive and caring. Prayer becomes fervent, desperate. "Give us this day our daily
bread—just today, Lord. Didn't He say to the psalmist,
'Call upon me in the day of trouble: I will deliver thee,
and thou shalt glorify me'?"

In one home the father prayed, "God, you fed two
thousand children in George Mueller's orphanage each
day. Surely you will also meet our needs."

There were answers to prayer. One family which had
been reduced to the last piece of bread prayed for food.
The father was ill and could eat only toasted white
bread, not the hard, heavy bread most families ate. The
next morning a friend brought him a little loaf. His wife
had been unable to find inner peace until she had sent
the bread to her neighbors.

One wonderful day, the word arrived that the Mennonites in the United States and Canada had heard of
their plight and were sending help. An American Mennonite Relief Administration committee had been organized and an appeal sent out to all Mennonites for
funds for relief for the Russian Mennonites. Carloads of
flour, clothing, and other foodstuffs were being sent.

Each day, the Russian Mennonites waited hungrily,
impatiently for AMRA, the forerunner of Mennonite
Central Committee, the inter-Mennonite relief agency,
to bring food.

"Daddy, we will soon get food from America, won't
we?" asked a little girl.

"Yes, my child, but now it is time to go to sleep."

"Daddy, when it comes we will get some soup from
the relief kitchen, won't we? Will the beggars get food
too?"

"I think so, but now go to sleep. We'll find out tomorrow."

The father and his two-year-old Irma spent many hours discussing the awaited food. All children knew the full details of who was sending the food, how it would be distributed, and so forth. Every bit of news sent new hope surging. Help was coming. People cared.

At last the AMRA relief kitchens were set up, but not before the cup of suffering had been filled. Though little Irma drew her parents' attention to the thought of food again and again, before it arrived, she died.

The day her spirit left her emaciated body, the sorrowing father wrote that only the nightingale's song had broken the stillness of that spring morning. Everywhere but in his heart peace had reigned, as he struggled to accept what God had allowed to happen. The state had told the people, "There is no God. There is no higher creative power. If someone talks to you about it, don't believe it!" Had their experience with Irma proved the truth of these hard words?

In February of 1922 workers from the United States and Canada, assisted by local Mennonites, set up food kitchens at various points. They distributed rations first to children, pregnant women, the sick and aged, and later to others. How wonderful to taste zwieback (traditional Mennonite rolls) and real bread again. They had almost forgotten how delicious bread smelled as it baked, let alone how to bake the old foods. They ate a strange-tasting soup called cocoa, and enjoyed oatmeal, rice, lard and beans.

Little Lena, who had sung for her supper, survived to praise God for caring friends. "Now thank we all our God, with heart and mouth and hands," she sang. Others ate their first meal of soup and bread baked with real white flour and could find only tears with which to say, "Thank you." It seemed impossible to believe they had escaped death.

"Good, dear 'mericans," said Lena, in her new hat, her stomach filled with cocoa and cookies.

"Thank you very much, you dear brothers and sisters in that faraway land for your love," wrote a father. "You showed a true spirit of compassion. The Lord will view what you have done for us as having been done to Him."

By May 1922 the kitchens were feeding 25,000 persons per day. The peak was reached in August when 40,000 rations were issued daily to all the hungry, regardless of nationality, race, or creed. The work continued for three years, although it declined after 1922.

By the fall of 1922 the harvest had increased, and many Mennonites no longer depended on the relief kitchens for food. Money provided by American Mennonites bought horses and cows so that farmers could return to the work they loved. Clothing arrived. Other relief agencies added their help.

By 1923, some of the Mennonites in Russia could see that the political situation there was not improving and that their religious freedom was not assured under the new communist government. They mustered enough courage to emigrate to Canada.

One who suffered much during the famine wrote that in years to come the children and grandchildren of the famine victims would continue to testify to the love they had received from America. Some of them are today testifying by taking part in Mennonite Disaster Service, helping others in the way they and their parents were once helped "in the name of Christ."

Chapter Seven

FROM PICNIC
TO INTERNATIONAL
ORGANIZATION

A family stopped by the Mennonite booth at the Kansas State Fair in Hutchinson.

"Mennonites? Who are they?" questioned the daughter.

Her father's reply was quick, "Mennonites are an outfit who go around doing good after floods and tornadoes."

He recognized MDS as the symbol by which non-Mennonites in increasing number know Mennonites in the twenty-five years since its inauspicious beginning at a Sunday school picnic in the summer of 1950.

Yet MDS began before that date in more casual ways. For generations mutual aid has been a principle practiced by Mennonites and Amish, as already related in the previous chapter. Although assistance was not limited to persons or families of like faith, yet because Mennonites were frequently isolated geographically and culturally from non-Mennonites, the latter were not as frequently recipients of this kind of caring concern.

Barn raising is probably the granddaddy of MDS. When a farmer's barn burned down or became too old or too small, his neighbors agreed on a day to build a new one. Sometimes a hundred men or more showed up, arriving in the early dawn. Often before the day was over a new barn had been built.

Older members of Kansas and Oklahoma communities remember that when a tornado struck, "the people from Kansas" came to help clean up. Assistance was spontaneous, unorganized, and unsophisticated.

By 1947 the Church of God in Christ, Mennonite (Holdeman) had established a continuing organization in time for cleanup after a tornado in Woodward, Oklahoma.

But at the picnic of young married couples from the Pennsylvania (now Whitestone) Mennonite Church in Hesston, Kansas, MDS as we now know it began to take shape and form.

Many of the people present were interested in continuing the positive witness to their neighbors which they had begun as conscientious objectors in Civilian Public Service during World War II. "A lot of our young men didn't serve in the war," explains one MDS unit coordinator. "Quite a few worked in hospitals and the like. Some went into the medical service, others into overseas relief. When they came back after the war, they asked themselves where they fit in, what they could do for society." Living in an area plagued by drought, tornadoes, and floods, they looked for a practical application of their Christian faith not only in time of national crisis but also in time of peace.

In the next weeks, they shared their convictions with members of a corresponding Sunday school class of the Hesston congregation at a joint meeting. The real enthusiam for this new venture burst forth at the informal discussion over refreshments after the meeting.

A committee was appointed consisting of Harold Dyck, Paul Shenk, and Allen Diller and the two teachers, Daniel Kauffman and Fred S. Brenneman.

The first step was to circulate a questionaire in the two Hesston congregations. What skills were available? Carpentry? Cooking? Typing? Welding? Nursing? Airplane piloting? Could the person come at a moment's notice? What equipment could each person furnish?

The new organization, which called itself the Mennonite Service Organization, named John Diller as the "stay-at-home" coordinator because he was confined to a wheelchair. He agreed to try. Nothing happened until May 17, 1951, when during a period of heavy rains, the Little Arkansas River flooded and Wichita called for help.

Lyle Yost, president of MSO, called Diller to tell him he was going to Wichita and that he should call volunteers to tell them to be ready to go.

"I didn't know how to do it," says Diller, "but I started calling people to get ready to go to Wichita."

About 6:00 p.m. Yost called again to say he had promised the officials fifteen men and one truck. "By eleven o'clock we had forty-five men and four trucks in Wichita," says Diller, "building sandbag dikes." A group of women also went to Wichita that night with sandwiches for the workers. By 6:00 a.m. they were released and went wearily home to face a day's work on the farm.

Marvin Hostetler, another of the early hardworking enthusiasts of the movement, says, "John Diller could relay what I (as field director) had said about need and the number of volunteers required. He was a coordinator in the true sense of the word. He could always come up with a volunteer."

A week after the Wichita flood a call came from Great Bend, Kansas, for help. Two carloads from Hesston went out to help, reinforced by another two carloads of young men from the Eden Mennonite Church at Moundridge. Here they carried sandbags through mud almost a foot deep to the dikes a couple hundred feet away. In Great Bend, as the volunteers worked, a big wedding dance was being celebrated in the city building. Very few men from the community were assisting at the dikes except those who were being paid by the city. One of the men who saw the volunteers struggling to maintain the dike looked at the armband with the initials MSO. He labeled the men the "Mighty Soaked Outfit." On another occasion they were called the "Midnight Service Organization."

Once in the early years one householder chased the volunteers from his yard because he didn't want sandbags scattered around his yard. At other times they faced the attitude, "Let the flood victims take care of themselves. They should have built on higher ground like I did away from the water."

As the floods worsened in Kansas in 1951, Mennonite churches sent volunteers to Marion, Florence, Kansas City, and Topeka for short-term cleanup.

About 150 men from at least twenty churches in four Mennonite conferences in Kansas and Nebraska worked through May 3, rebuilding flood-damaged houses and the St. Mark's African Methodist Episcopal Church in Topeka. Other persons went to Topeka for one day's service. A number of women helped hang wallpaper and painted.

The Red Cross furnished materials for repair of five houses and room and board for the men. All the houses needed cleaning, Sheetrock on the walls and ceilings, new floors, papering, and painting. One small house, belonging to a woman in her eighties, was so badly damaged it was completely replaced.

"The house split at the gables when we started jacking it up," said a volunteer. "We built her a two-room house. She really wanted her old house back, but it wasn't possible to repair it."

"A lot of people appreciated the fact that we came to work for no pay," he recalled, "but they didn't understand it."

The Topeka reconstruction was the largest project of this kind attempted by Kansas Mennonites. But new challenges awaited them which forced the new movement into greater growth.

In March 1952, after a tornado swept through White County, Arkansas, Peter Dyck, pastor of the Eden Mennonite Church, Moundridge, questioned, "What are we going to do about Arkansas?" John Diller, as coordinator, agreed to write a letter to the Mennonite churches in Central Kansas if Dyck would chair the meeting. Dyck agreed.

On March 31, 1952, representatives of the MCC-constituency churches within a forty-mile radius of Hesston met to discuss the disaster in Arkansas and whether it would not be well for them "to organize and be ready to step right into a disaster area and go to work as a unit, rather than to go in as small groups, independent of each other, yet all under the name Mennonite."

Eighty men representing twenty-eight congregations from four Mennonite conferences attended the meeting. The chairman read from James 2: 26, "For as the body without the spirit is dead, so faith without works is dead also." Then he reported on the work of various relief and service organizations during the past year—flood evacuations, sandbagging, and flood rehabilitation.

According to the minutes of the meeting, it was the general feeling that Mennonites should unite under one organization so that they could work more effectively, devoting less time and money to administration and more to service. It was further pointed out that relief organizations and city officials preferred to work with one body which represented all groups rather than with a number of small organizations.

The new disaster committee consisted of two men from each branch of the MCC-constituent churches which wanted to cooperate. They were instructed not to take the place of existing relief committees, brotherhoods, and service organizations, but to provide help to them as needed. And the committee was not to solicit funds outside church channels. The committee sent a

MDS rescues a family stranded by a flood at Newton, Kansas, in the early 1950s.

representative to the Arkansas storm area to study what emergency relief was needed.

After April 7, the Church of God in Christ, Mennonite volunteers from four states who had gone to Arkansas on their own initiative phased out their work in the Arkansas storm cleanup. At once the temporary disaster committee sent ninety-three men to Judsonia, Arkansas, for short-term work and arranged for longer-term rehabilitation of eight houses belonging to the aged, widowed, or handicapped.

For the next few years, the disaster committee mobilized at least once a year to help in major disasters in Kansas, Oklahoma, and Nebraska.

The committee tried to establish a contact man other than the pastor in each congregation. Whenever word came of a disaster, Diller telephoned every Mennonite church in the state to gather volunteers. He also maintained a list of equipment available from chain saws to boats to generators.

"Those were the days of the old crank phones with the local operator who said, 'Number please,' " said Diller. "I used to be on the phone for four hours straight calling Kansas congregations." Even the girls in the exchange office learned to speed his work. He would give them a list of four or five numbers and they would have the next person on the line by the time he was finished with the first one. "We never came up very short of volunteers," he said. "Many times we went way over our goal."

The first years were busy with disasters and with learning experiences for the MDS workers. In 1953, Galen Rudiger, with H. B. Schmidt, went to Hebron, Nebraska, to attend a meeting with Red Cross and city officials to discuss how best to meet the needs of the people after a tornado. They spent the night in the mayor's home and together they worked until late into the night organizing the activities of MDS volunteers the next day. But at other projects the same approach of simply contacting the mayor didn't work.

During a week of MDS operations in Meeker, Oklahoma in 1954 a good relationship developed between the Tabor Mennonite Church, north of Newton, Kansas, and the Meeker Christian Church, in whose building meals for the volunteers were served. Here they were asked questions which they would be asked later at most places about themselves as Mennonites.

"Do you believe in God?" asked the people of Meeker.

"Yes."

"We do too."

Finally one of the local persons suggested, "We believe the same things. Why have different denominations?"

H. B. Schmidt, pastor of the Tabor church, responded that some people like red apples and some yellow, some like their apples sweet and some sour, but they are all apples. So with churches. Some prefer one, some another, but they are all Christian. The friendship between the two churches continued beyond the disaster period, with the entire congregations exchanging visits on occasion.

The following years kept the Kansas MDS busy. A tornado in Udall, Kansas, in May 1955 killed seventy persons, completely destroyed 173 homes, and damaged sixteen others. It brought out 1,100 volunteers with trucks on Memorial Day. They combed through the wreckage looking for watches, money, and valuables, even false teeth, before the debris was pushed together and loaded into trucks by army equipment.

On the same day the tornado hit Udall, another tornado struck near Blackwell, Oklahoma. Other Kansas volunteers cleared boards and other debris from farmland on which crops were only a few days away from harvest. Forty-five farms were affected in a mile-wide

101

strip twenty miles long.

From the early days of the movement, MDS workers ate with Red Cross volunteers and used Red Cross cots at night.

By the time MDS arrived after the Galveston, Texas, hurricane, in 1966, Red Cross officials were looking for MDS. They said, "These are the people we told you were coming."

The definition of disaster was expanded to include the chronic as well as the acute crisis, destruction caused not only by nature, but also by acts of man. MDS (Regions II and III) was the first disaster organization to send workers to repair houses in urban low-income areas, when it began working with Jeff-Vander-Lou, Inc., in St. Louis in 1967.

At present, community work, assisting disabled and disadvantaged persons, aiding in Headstart programs, and caring for disadvantaged children are all becoming worthy projects. Inner-city work, rehabilitating ghetto homes, continues to be an important aspect of MDS work.

The organization which began so small grew as its activities increased. A headquarters was established at Hesston. Training schools for field directors were begun in 1955. A mobile office was added in 1956. The film *El Dorado* was produced in 1958. Rescue teams were trained and assembled in 1959. Radio equipment was added in 1960.

The program that had begun in Kansas didn't stay there, however. It was an idea whose time has come. Other states and Canadian provinces organized MDS units patterned after the Kansas model as the need arose.

Units formed along geographic lines. Pennsylvania organized in 1955 when it was struck by the Stroudsburg floods. Six or seven small settlement and outpost communities in South Carolina organized a state unit after

Mennonite volunteers help clear fallen debris following a hurricane in the Gulfport, Mississippi area in 1969.

tornadoes hit in 1973. In Minnesota, where Mennonites are concentrated in the extreme north and south, two units formed. At Kalispell, Montana, one congregation maintains its own unit because it is 350 miles away from the nearest Mennonite church. Pennsylvania has six units because of its large concentration of Mennonites. Three eastern Tennessee congregations joined the North Carolina unit because they are closer to them than other Mennonite churches in their state.

The island of Puerto Rico with 14 congregations is organizing an individual unit.

Canada

In Canada the pattern of development was much the same. Dating such beginnings is difficult since a spontaneous response to various needs often preceded all but the loosest kind of organization as it did in the United States.

Although natural disasters played a midwife's role in the birth of MDS in Canada, another motivation looms large in the records. During the early sixties, Canada was still preoccupied with the possibility of a nuclear holocaust. Civil defense was a continuing concern of the federal government. Later the Emergency Measures Organization was formed to care for civil defense needs as well as to deal with other types of emergencies.

Although Mennonites were in accord with many of the objectives of these two organizations, they also had qualms about being identified with government or military responses. Thus it was natural in Canada to find the Historic Peace Church Council of Canada (HPCCC) fathering MDS.

In 1956 HPCCC hosted sixty delegates in Winnipeg to consider greater coordination of MDS on a national basis. By the spring of 1958, British Columbia, Manitoba, and Ontario, the provinces with the largest concentration of Mennonites, had organized formally.

Later units formed also in Saskatchewan and Alberta. The final organization of MDS (Canada) under HPCCC came in October of 1961.

Actually, MDS (Canada) maintains an odd stance within two organizations. Canada is labeled Region V in the North American Mennonite Disaster Service organization. (See Appendix C.) As one of the five regions under the MDS banner, the Canadian organization functions as part of the whole with only minor representation on the governing body. Although Canada represents more than twenty-five percent of the North American Mennonite constituency, it has only three representatives on the MDS international board of eighteen.

However, this imbalance matters little in the functioning of MDS (Canada). It is simply another way by which MCC responds to a special kind of emergency. Responsibility for funding is carried by MCC with money released as requested according to need. Local MDS units are autonomous, as they are in the United States. Area or provincial MDSers respond to needs according to local needs and resources.

MDS units in Canada have never had a strong sense of belonging to each other. Disasters have generally been south of the border. Help has flowed again and again to United States communities. Only occasionally has reciprocity been experienced.

However, in spite of its unique characteristics, MDS (Canada) is alive and well. In 1974, a Monday holiday call in Ontario raised 120 volunteers for flooding in Bridgeport and 400 volunteers for Cambridge to assist in flood cleanup operations. And that after 350 volunteers had worked on the Sunday preceding.

In 1974 in Moose Jaw, Saskatchewan, thirty volunteers came out each day even though the area is sparsely settled by Mennonites compared to southern Manitoba or Ontario. Rivers in the area had become raging torrents, flooding surrounding communities.

Two flood experiences in southern Manitoba during the spring of 1974 were covered by volunteers from the province.

International Organization

Mennonite Central Committee, the inter-Mennonite relief agency, called the first wide-scale meeting of interested people on March 2, 1955, in Chicago. There the representatives of regional groups adopted the proposal that a national coordination committee be established composed of one representative from each of the constituent groups.

In 1961 a young attorney by the name of Wayne Clemens,* was hired by the national committee as executive coordinator, and by 1962, Mennonite Disaster Service had become a section of MCC, a relief and service agency with agriculture, education, and health programs in thirty-eight countries.

Mennonite Disaster Service currently involves more than 1,900 Mennonite and Brethren in Christ congregations which are divided into 270 zones, fifty-two units (forty-six in the United States, five in Canada, one in Honduras), and five regions (four in the United States, one in Canada). (See Appendix C.)

The paid staff totals one person; all others volunteer their time. The organizational structure on any level,

---

*Wayne Clemens, now practicing law in Souderton, Pennsylvania, served as half-time MDS executive coordinator from 1962-65 to fulfill his I-W assignment. Previous to that C.L. Graber of Goshen, Indiana, served for six months to set up the structure when MDS was officially made part of MCC. Harry Martens, now with Mennonite Foundation in the Central states and a veteran MCC relief worker, served from 1954 to 1961 as national and international MDS coordinator on a volunteer basis. Executive coordinators since Clemens' time have been Delmar Stahly and C. Nelson Hostetter.

whether regional, national, or international, is maintained to serve a supportive and coordinating role rather than an administrative one. No orders come from the top, only guidelines for program planning and project operations.

The governing body of Mennonite Disaster Service is the MDS section of MCC which has eighteen members representing major Mennonite groups and includes the five regional directors. The section meets twice each year and elects an executive committee of five from among themselves to meet three to five times a year.

All local MDS units remain autonomous and arrive at their own decisions and formation of policy according to local needs. Each unit has a roster of officers, the chairman being responsible for the overall operations. The secretary-treasurer is assigned the listing of active congregational contact persons and raising basic finances and keeping records, not always considered important at first. "We just went out to work and then came home and plowed," said one coordinator.

The coordinator's duties are to relay information from the field director through the network to the congregations to set in motion the necessary logistics and to alert volunteers.

The MDS service roster reads like a roll call of national disasters. Name the disaster and you'll find MDS was there. Nor has MDS stayed in traditional Mennonite areas or concerned itself solely with floods and tornadoes. Hurricanes, earthquakes, drought conditions, bombings caused by racial disturbances, have all brought MDS into action.

After twenty-five years of service throughout the United States and Canada, and even in other countries, the picnic-type organization has long been left behind, and not without regrets.

Elmer Ediger, speaker at the 25th anniversary observance of MDS at Hesston, Kansas, in February

1975, said, "It has been as spontaneous a movement as we have had. It has shown that ordinary people, if they are dedicated and put in a place of need, can do great things."

As MDS continues its extended operations which expose Mennonites and their service to the general public, it has two fears. The first of these is that praise may rob the organization of its spirit of servanthood.

Robert Schrag editorialized in *Mennonite Weekly Review,* "Probably no other Mennonite endeavor has received as much local and national press coverage—all of it favorable. The sight of a host of volunteers in work clothes coming at short notice from distant points to donate time and labor to complete strangers—that always makes news. Good news."

"Yet servanthood is one of the hallmarks of Christ's kingdom, where greatness is determined by the willingness to be servant of all," reminded Peter J. Dyck, the first chairman, at this 25th anniversary meeting.

But the second fear is an equally gnawing one: that the trend from charisma toward bureaucracy, which is the normal sequence in any organization or institution, will cause MDS to become brittle and lose its original vigor and vitality.

MDS wants only to remain an organization of the people for the people—to the glory of God. "The volunteer should be given first place," says Diller, as one who has watched the little movement expand into the extensive service organization MDS is today. "All others only help to keep the road maintained so that the volunteer can get out to the fellow who needs his assistance."

Chapter Eight

MDS
GOES OVERSEAS

In 1961 Mennonite Disaster Service went international for the first time.

It happened quickly. Men were working overseas for the first time before anyone could caution against it or against the precedent this action might be setting.

On October 31, 1961, Hurricane Hattie hit British Honduras, now Belize, full force. At once Jacob M. Klassen, Mennonite Central Committee assistant director of foreign relief and services, asked for a dozen men to spend two months building some temporary houses.

"Let's give them a hand," said C. L. Graber, MDS national coordinator at the time. Word went out across North America to Mennonite churches that help was needed in British Honduras.

Church bulletins pleaded: "Many people are homeless in British Honduras. Their houses have been smashed or washed away by a hurricane. Builders are needed now. Who can go?"

One month after the initial call, twenty-eight volunteers from eight Mennonite groups and ten states and provinces were "giving a hand" in the midst of the smelly wreckage left behind by Hattie.

British Honduras
British Honduras, now Belize, is a seventy-mile-wide strip of semi-tropical land adhering for 175 miles to the

underside of the Yucatan fishhook-shaped peninsula. Its south side is washed by the Caribbean Sea, much of it only a few feet above sea level. Belize, the capital city, was built on this low coastland.

This little country is not on the beaten path of international trade and travel. "If the world had any ends," wrote Aldous Huxley in 1930, "British Honduras would be one of them. It is not on the way from anywhere to anywhere else."

The country is small—about the size of Massachusetts. The population in 1960 was 90,000, including Indians, Negroes, Spanish, and other racial driftwood. Yet into this multiracial picture came still another ethnic group in 1958, three years before Hattie struck. One thousand Mennonites migrated from the extreme north of Mexico into the British Colony, settling in three communities inland.

A little later Mennonite Central Committee opened a center in Belize, which provided an outlet for produce the Mennonite colonists brought to the city. Still later, missionaries from the Eastern Mennonite Board at Salunga, Pennsylvania, arrived, and the MCC personnel were transferred to that organization. So later when the hurricane struck, missionary officials and MDS worked together to arrange for volunteers to enter the country.

The first report of Hurricane Hattie came from Chester and Vivian Denlinger, who were living at the Belize Center. "The breeze," they wrote, "turned into a strong wind just after midnight. Rain started coming in and the windows upstairs gave way. We heard loud thumpings and we thought our roof was falling in, and when we heard the crash of our next-door neighbor's house, we had prayer . . . ."

Hurricane Hattie hit Belize on Tuesday, October 31, 1961, with a twenty-foot wall of water. With no natural or artificial barriers to contain it, the Caribbean came crashing into the city, where more than one third of the

Peter Dueck, a Mennonite from Belize, working on a house in El Progreso with two Hondurans.

population of the country lived.

Big houses were moved from their foundations and left leaning at crazy angles. Little houses were demolished. Debris, drowned chickens, and people floated around in ten feet of water. When the water subsided, deep ooze and refuse covered the city. Looting was rampant.

Not all deaths were caused by drowning. Sheets of tin roofing ripped away by the storm's winds accounted for many of the approximately three hundred deaths. Victims were buried quickly in a common grave to forestall an epidemic.

About one month later, twenty-eight MDS volunteers from the United States and Canada arrived to help construct temporary buildings for those left homeless by the storm and to repair salvageable structures.

The team members took applications from persons without resources. From these they selected the families in greatest need of immediate help. Much of this help involved putting houses back on their foundations and replacing roofs.

The men worked with refugees as much as possible and also helped to rebuild damaged churches, regardless of faith or creed.

One of the men wrote home: "Our first impression was, 'What a mess. How can we help?' Our spirits were revived when we attended a Christian church where all present were dark-skinned people. The adverse conditions did not hinder the spirit of worship. These people sang from the heart, 'Blessed Assurance' and 'How Firm a Foundation.' Their happy faces and their thank-you's really challenged us."

Another man wrote: "The relationship and fellowship between our workers and the townspeople has been good. We are making many friends."

Because of the almost complete devastation of Belize, the government decided to rebuild the capital about thirty-two miles inland on a higher elevation. Until plans for this relocation were finalized, a temporary city was needed. About sixteen miles inland, halfway between Belize and the proposed new site, a village of temporary, army-like barracks was erected, mainly by MDS labor. The government named the makeshift city Hattieville in grim remembrance of the storm that had destroyed Belize. In 1970 the new capital was completed and named Belmopan.

When the MDS teams left the country, the governor thanked them personally. One old lady said, "I never knew there were such kind people in the world."

Haiti and Hurricane Flora

The destruction caused by hurricanes Flora and Inez on the island of Haiti gave MDS another opportunity for international service.

Both storms set out in the usual northeasterly course of hurricanes across the Americas. Their births in the South Atlantic conformed to tradition. But it soon became evident that Flora (and then Inez) was bent on making an outstanding reputation for herself. Both chalked up some all-time records in destruction.

Flora battered Haiti for nine hours with 140-mile winds on October 3, 1963. She spun inside Cuba for five straight days giving Cuba the longest beating any hurricane ever inflicted. Her stalling tactics made her doubly destructive. She lacked a definite steering pattern. *The New York Times* commented: "Flora took her place in history as the most deadly storm ever to come from the tropical Atlantic."

The densely populated areas of the Haitian peninsula and the eastern half of Cuba took the brunt of the hurricane. The southern peninsula of Haiti, and Petit Goave, forty miles still farther south, fared badly. In Cote de Fer, on the southern coast, practically all homes were destroyed and many people were killed or injured.

Transportation and communication between the devastated areas had broken down.

The World Health Organization estimated the dead at 5,000 and the homeless at 100,000. Coffee, rice, and banana plantations were wiped out in Flora's twenty-four-hour rampage. Dr. Gerard Phileppeau, Haitian minister of health, described Haiti as a "sodden trash heap, with towns ravished."

The president of the Haitian Red Cross commented, "You just don't see any people. Where towns and villages stood, you can't find the bodies; they are buried in the mud and debris, or were washed away by the sea."

Both countries (Cuba and Haiti) were poverty-stricken even before the ordeals of the storm. Both were ruled by dictators—Haiti by Dr. Francois "Papa" Duvalier, Cuba by communist Fidel Castro—whose political pride kept them from accepting humanitarian offers from the American government and the American Red Cross. Relations of these Caribbean leaders with the United States was at a low ebb at this time.

Although Haitian officials requested helicopters from the United States to survey the damage, they refused all other kinds of aid unless it came from private organizations or individuals. Fidel Castro said emphatically, "For us, all offers of help from the United States, official or semiofficial, are hypocritical." Cuban exiles were streaming into the United States at the time. And so this attitude made it easier for the American Quakers and MDS to get into Haiti.

MDS was also welcomed into Haiti because MCC Voluntary Service personnel (somewhat similar to Peace Corps) had already been working in the poverty-rich country for several years. Eleven members were located at Hospital Albert Schweitzer in Saint Marc and eight at the MCC-operated hospital at Grande Riviere du Nord. In addition to carrying on medical

114

work at these two places, the VSers participated in community development projects.

So MDS had almost an open door before them when they came to Haiti. Neither the national nor international Red Cross was on the scene. Not even the United States Agency for International Development (USAID), which usually participates in emergency operations, was present. And the government of Haiti had virtually no facilities for responding to catastrophes of this kind.

MDS took quick steps to recruit volunteers for a reconstruction team. Fifteen builders responded from eight states. Less than one month after Hurricane Flora's visit, the volunteers set foot in the storm-ravished Cote de Fer. A shipment of 150 tons of building supplies accompanied them.

Another five Mennonites were sent at the same time to serve with Church World Service in an agricultural program involving seed planting. Arlin Hunsberger, VS director, was named overall director in Haiti and Jacob Nauman, project foreman.

In November, two nurses and one doctor joined the MDS units and the other doctors working with Church World Service. By November 29 each doctor's team had held approximately one thousand consultations and had administered four thousand immunizations. Travel for these medical teams was sometimes a three-to-four-hour mule ride. Yet this endeavor gave a real boost to the scattered evangelical Christians in the area who were delighted by the Protestant medical team.

The assignment at Cote de Fer for the MDS builders was a difficult one. The builders, as well as the medical team, established a tent camp since no local housing was available. Lack of communication and regular transportation made life more complicated. If trucks were available, the MDS teams had no gas; when gas arrived, the trucks had moved elsewhere. Overland transportation was impossible. Building supplies and food were brought to Cote de Fer from Port-au-Prince.

The volunteers daily faced the frustrations caused by culture shock and language barriers in addition to the threat of illness and the inconveniences of camp living. The sudden change of climate and diet easily upset the delicate balance of the body. Tropical humidity and heat induced drowsiness and a general feeling of disinterest. Unfamiliar sights and smells, especially in a setting of ugly poverty, promoted nausea. When strange food caused stomach cramps, ambition to work fled.

One of the builders wrote, "Life in the disaster zone is far rougher than many volunteers had imagined. Some of the Mennonite volunteers in Cote de Fer are housed in a local jail. The destruction and poverty are indescribable."

The builders worked at the construction of multiple family homes, using homemade concrete blocks and corrugated steel roofing. Local help was utilized by enlisting those who were to occupy the houses and by providing food for those who were willing to work. The men discovered that what had been considered laziness was more often weakness caused by hunger. One foreman discovered that even a little candy brought extra dividends in work accomplished.

Gravel was hauled one mile up the river, some by donkey, some by women carrying it in dishpans. Everything else was carried either by shovel or by two hand trucks made by the MDS director. By North American standards progress was slow, but eventually concrete block buildings began to rise where a village had been virtually wiped out.

One of the workers shared some of his day-to-day experiences: "Our meals are getting better since meat is more plentiful. The cook can only prepare what he has. Rice and beans are still our main meal. . . . It is hard to sit down to a big meal and have sixteen or twenty

Haitians gathering around to watch us eat and they have nothing, not even a house to go into. As I write this letter, I see a family of five sitting on the foundation where their home once was. They do their cooking and eating without walls or roof. . . .

Those men in small boats wanted to sell wood carvings and dishes. I have never seen people so desperate to sell and get money as here. . . .

This tent living may have been all right for Abraham, but I am getting tired of it. . . . There are so many dogs around here, especially in the kitchen. I have seen only one cat. But the chickens started laying eggs in our tents. This dinner a cluck with seven chicks arrived at camp . . . also a lot of small pigs and goats. . . . We had plenty of meat today; they brought four turkeys for our Thanksgiving dinner. We had one prepared the native way. It tasted like they must have forgot to take the insides out. . . .

"We have plenty of food, but my clothes are getting bigger. The wash ladies are sure hard on our clothes. They take them to the river to wash. They lay the clothes on a board and hit them with a stone till they are clean. . . . The water was too rough to unload the ship. I told Pastor Lacome we would rather not work on Sunday. He said the Bible says, 'If the ox falls into the well, we should help him out.' So we decided two men would help him. But one got sick and the sea got too rough, so the Lord won again."

One evening a group of builders out walking came to the hut of an eighty-six-year-old widow whose thatched roof had been leaking. They measured the hut, returned home for some lumber and tin, and came back. By five o'clock she had a new tin roof on her house. Sam Miller writes: "She was so happy she wept. She said she had had a vision that the Lord would send someone to fix her roof. Many people watch us on every job. I believe they are impressed with this expression of concern. Plans are

117

to construct a small clinic and some more small houses."

When the MDS unit first came to Cote de Fer they found guards walking around with guns. Years of colonialism had made the nationals suspicious of white men, but when they found out why the MDSers had come, their attitude changed, even toward the government.

The great poverty and hunger of the Haitians haunted the MDS teams each day. Twelve-to-fourteen-year-old boys who worked for the men begged to be taken back to the United States to get an education. Women even offered them their babies so that the little ones would have a chance for a better life. Petty theft was common in order to stay alive. By the time the unit left, they had given away much of their own clothing. One boy who had begged for a new hat, after receiving it, came back the next day with some eggs in appreciation.

One volunteer said, "We felt that although we had sacrificed to come, breaking some business appointments, this was an experience we would not have missed for anything."

As in the United States, MDS units often closed the day's activities with group singing. An audience of local children and adults watched them. Then later in the evening, when they had retired, the voodoo drums beat their messages into the darkness of the tropical night. Local dogs, determined to outdo them, howled even louder, both sounds reminding the MDSers that the great poverty was exceeded by the greater spiritual need.

After four months of disaster service activities, in which thirty-five men and two women were part of the MDS unit at Cote de Fer and Petit Goave, the time came to leave. But first they were granted opportunity to meet with the national leaders.

The volunteers had a fifty-five-minute private audience with President Duvalier on March 3 in the Yellow room of the palace. Health Minister Phileppeaux arranged the audience and coached the men on proper decorum. Three of his office staff were temporarily relieved of their coats and ties so that the casually dressed MDS men would be properly attired.

At the interview, a photo album illustrating the rebuilding project at Cote de Fer was presented to the president. He requested that these pictures be shown on television so that his people could see what the foreigners had accomplished in their country. He thanked the men for their services.

On March 4, Church World Service and MDS received citations of honor. Minister Phileppeaux said in his speech he had known the president for fifteen years and this was the first time he had found Duvalier satisfied. Haiti had had its share of problems with foreigners, including Americans. However, the Mennonite volunteers were the most welcome foreigners in Haiti. The president urged the men to continue the kind of work they had been doing and to "invade" his country with an even larger program.

Haiti and Hurricane Inez

Three years later when Hurricane Inez struck Haiti, MDS found that President Duvalier was still of the same mind. He and his Minister of Health were now asking—and urging—the MDS men to work on restoring government buildings.

Inez moved with diabolical vengeance in September of 1966. She hit Guadeloupe, the Virgin Islands, Puerto Rico, and the Dominican Republic. Haiti came next. After losing a bit of strength over Cuba, she regained it as she neared Florida, then backtracked into the Gulf of Mexico, damaging Florida with only fringe gales.

Hurricane Inez reached back and slapped Cuba again, then set a straight course for the Yucatan peninsula of Mexico, which she hit with a glancing blow. Bottled up now in the western Gulf of Mexico, she turned toward the Texas coast and Galveston, then veered westward toward the Mexican city of Tampico.

A day later, Inez headed northward again for Texas at Brownsville. Erratic to the end, she veered once more and slammed into the Mexican mainland, where she died. Even in her death throes, the hurricane leveled two towns, leaving 30,000 persons homeless and doing $12 million damage. Inez set a record as the longest-lived of all hurricanes—eighteen continuous days.

The coastline of Haiti had once again suffered much damage. President Duvalier's insistent request was complimentary to the MDS volunteers, yet it countered the basic MDS policy of extending help in a person-to-person relationship. The aim of MDS is to help poor people, not poor governments. It took considerable diplomacy to explain this policy to the Haitian government.

This second Haiti disaster alerted MDS officials to the need to keep its relationship to other organizations in clear perspective. One relief agency cannot operate independently in a disaster area. Cooperation, not competition, must prevail. On the other hand, MDS learned that an agency, especially a Christian one, dare not become so merged with other agencies that it loses its identity and Christian witness. It is one thing to work with another agency, another to work for it.

Yet in spite of problems regarding relationships with governments and inter-organizational relationships, in spite of work slowdowns, in spite of difficulties of cultural adjustments, two MDS teams served more than a month each to restore the two villages, Jacmel and Marigot, hardest hit by the hurricane. The men built dozens of cement blockhouses and taught the Haitians to build more.

When the period of service ended, national MDS coordinator Delmar Stahly said, "The working together of Haitians and MDS men and the increasing appreciation of understanding developing between peoples of varying cultures are very significant. . . . Although we had hoped to provide more shelters for Haitians, our primary purpose was the person-to-person contacts, the witnessing to our faith, and the serving of needy people in the name of Christ."

Assistant director Jake Dyck, added, "What the men receive and take home means as much as what they do here."

Managua, Nicaragua

Most of the 450,000 inhabitants of Managua, the capital of Nicaragua, had hung up their Christmas decorations the evening of December 23, 1972, before retiring. That night, approximately six thousand men, women, and children were killed when walls and roofs fell in on them as they slept. About 250,000 persons were made homeless instantly by an earthquake. Ninety percent of the business area was destroyed. Outside the city minimum damage occurred.

The *New York Times* reported that by Christmas Eve, twenty-four hours after the earthquake hit, 1,000 bodies had already been buried in a mass grave. Christmas Day dawned with five times that many bodies still covered by a sea of rubble. The dollar damage was estimated at $800 million. In seconds, the city of Managua had been shaken to pieces like a fragile ornament in the hands of a capricious child, the prospects for a joyous Christmas shattered, and the prevailing poverty of the land compounded by this new calamity.

Nicaragua is a country in Central America of about two million people. The majority are poor farmers. During the rainy season of 1971 very little rain fell. As a result, crops were poor. The rainy season of 1972 brought even less rain. The harvest that year was slimmer than the year before. By December 1972 many people were suffering from the effects of malnutrition.

121

The earthquake added new heavy burdens to a people unable to carry those they already had.

Yet the response of those who offered aid matched the magnitude of the disaster. The *Reader's Digest* rated the outpouring of relief as "one of the biggest humanitarian operations of recent times." Even the Cuban government overlooked its past differences with Nicaragua and sent help for humanitarian reasons. Private and religious agencies contributed cash and personnel. Mennonite Central Committee and Mennonite Disaster Service jointly responded to the disaster. And once again a natural catastrophe became the opportunity for Mennonites to move close together in a cooperative effort.

Three MCC-constituency conferences were already in Nicaragua at the time of the earthquake. They had operated independent missions in the country for some years. These three missions (Evangelical Mennonite, Steinbach, Manitoba; Conservative Mennonite, Irwin, Ohio; and Brethren in Christ, Elizabethtown, Pennsylvania) formed a Field Advisory Committee and invited MCC/MDS to set up and administer a relief program. The first links in the chain of help needed to administer relief in Nicaragua had been joined.

Often in overseas countries, various denominations operate mission activities, but independently of one another. The earthquake brought the other evangelical missions in Nicaragua together in a program of assistance. An international committee of twenty Protestant groups called Commité Evangelico Para Ayudar Desorallos (CEPAD)—(Evangelical Committee to Help Refugees) was formed for the emergency operation, headed by an able and dedicated Baptist pastor, Dr. Gustav Parejon.

The Mennonite Field Advisory Committee cooperated with this new committee, as did other international voluntary agencies, to make the distribu-

Feliciano and Noel, members of a Nicaraguan Mennonite church, sift gravel for home construction following the massive destruction of their country's capital city, Managua, in December 1972.

tion of relief goods pouring into the country more efficient. By special permission of President A. Somoza of Nicaragua, material goods donated by evangelicals in other countries could be distributed directly by this committee without first passing through government hands.

At first the only funds available were $10,000 pledged from the MCC emergency fund. Like the loaves and fishes Christ fed the multitudes, this $10,000 grew to more than $150,000 in addition to much material aid. Without any specific general appeal for funds, the Mennonite and Brethren in Christ constituency responded with $35,000. Through MCC (Canada) $25,000 was received from the Canadian International Development Agency, matched by $7,500 from Canadian Mennonite resources. Finally the Lilly Foundation came forward with $50,000 to permit a more extended effort. Two hundred students of the Goshen College student study program who had been in Nicaragua before the earthquake raised $40,000 in a special effort.

Many individuals volunteered themselves as well as their money. Twenty-four volunteers served two months or more. Construction workers were recruited through MDS, while community social workers arrived from Goshen College and the constituent missions.

Edgar Stoesz,* who administered the Managua relief program from the MCC home base at Akron, Pennsylvania, commented, "It has been most heartwarming to see how spontaneously the Mennonite Church has responded to another disaster. For every worker who was assigned, at least five applied." The relief projects of this cooperating group of missionaries, MDS

---

*Edgar Stoesz, MCC director for Latin America, administered the Managua relief program from MCC's head office in Pennsylvania. Arthur Driedger served as temporary field director for the MCC/MDS activities in Nicaragua. MDS international coordinator, Nelson Hostetter, recruited volunteers from the home constituency.

workers, and others varied according to need. MCC personnel fed up to 17,000 people daily with the help of CEPAD and supplies donated by the United States and Canadian governments. Four hundred new wooden houses were built at an average cost of $212.75; others were repaired. Some temporary classroom facilities were constructed.

Assistance was given to Nueva Guinea, a new colonization region of 1,500 families which included quake victims; to ALFALIT, the Protestant-sponsored literacy program; to Provadencia; a Baptist-supported agency sponsoring some lay clinics for low income families, and to various spiritual ministries.

"Managua is a 1973 affirmation," Stoesz concluded, "that the world has not been overtaken by calloused hearts and compassion fatigue. People gave generously of themselves and their substance so that the burdens of those who suffered this tragedy could be lightened. To God be the glory!"

Chapter Nine

BEHIND
THE IRON CURTAIN

In 1963 Mennonite Disaster Service took the next step. It pushed behind the Iron Curtain into communist territory. Six men—three Mennonites and three Church of the Brethren—went to Skopje, Yugoslavia, for two months following its devastation by an earthquake to build houses and to build bridges between countries with differing ideologies.

An earthquake hit Skopje, the second largest city in Yugoslavia, the morning of Friday, July 26, 1963. By evening the fragmented news reached the outside world: eighty percent of Skopje's buildings were totally or partially destroyed.

Eighty miles to the south of the city, John Wieler, director of the Mennonite Central Committee project at Nomos Pellas in Macedonia, Greece, received the garbled news. By five o'clock the next morning he and an assistant were on their way to Skopje to survey the damage and to find out if MCC could help. Visas into the country were granted free of charge.

In the central part of the city the men saw damaged buildings everywhere. They could only spot one unscathed building. Giant cracks, two of them sixty feet long and four feet wide, threatened the shattered city with earth slides and cave-ins.

All of Skopje's 170,000 citizens had moved out into the open and settled in parks and boulevards. A bewildered atmosphere prevailed. Refugee-like columns of people were leaving the city by bicycle, truck, and bus. Many people sat dazed beside large piles of rubble that only hours ago had been their homes, anguish and grief etched on every line of their faces. Under the rubble still lay the bodies of missing relatives.

The two MCC men learned that the officials estimated two thousand persons had died in the quake. Emergency relief action had already begun. The Red Cross was functioning. People were rescuing possessions from partly damaged buildings. Survivors were being sought. City officials had set up a central control station and all high government officials, including Marshal Tito, had arrived in the city. The second day after the earthquake, heavy equipment such as dozers, cranes, Michigan loaders, and mining trucks had been pressed into service.

How could MCC help?

The answer was hard to find in the general confusion and with the language difficulties at central control. But the men didn't give up. Although inexperienced in emergency relief work, John Wieler felt sure MCC personnel could help clear rubble and reconstruct homes, perhaps through another agency.

The push to help the disaster-struck people behind the Iron Curtain moved from Europe across the Atlantic to the MCC head office at Akron, Pennsylvania. Should MCC continue its efforts to get into Yugoslavia? The response was quick and positive. Go ahead. Use American personnel, or even European Mennonites to help in the Skopje disaster. One thousand dollars was made immediately available for the project.

But even that positive word didn't open the doors.

In the days that followed, the city, government, and Red Cross officials and other service and church agencies in Skopje gave MCC personnel a sympathetic ear, but no assurance of actually getting their workers into the country. They encouraged MCC to help Protestant churches gather $500,000 to purchase more than one hundred prefabricated houses to replace those destroyed in the earthquake.

But MCC personnel in Europe weren't satisfied with only donating money. "If we really wish to influence these people," said John Wieler, "it must be by personal contact. I feel we need to offer help in a way that necessitates sending a representative."

He suggested a team of skilled craftsmen. "Perhaps I am thinking about an International Mennonite Disaster Service," he said. "Once in a country, invaluable contacts and friendships certainly could lead to other opportunities to witness to Him in whose name we serve."

The next step was to contact the World Council of Churches (WCC) in Geneva, offering MCC manpower to assist in the erection of houses in Skopje. It was clear that Yugoslavia would need help from outside its borders to do some of the reconstruction. But the response was negative.

But MCC did not take even that discouraging reply as the final answer. They still hoped and prayed that a few of the men on the Protestant contingent that was to build the prefabricated houses in Skopje would be Mennonites. And then suddenly the door which had been shut so tightly, swung open.

On September 4, the Frankfurt MCC office received a call from WCC in Geneva that it was providing six builders for the prefabricated houses. Mennonite Disaster Service in the United States was being given the responsibility of recruiting three of them and the Brethren Service Commission the other three.

MDS was in—behind the Iron Curtain for the first time.

A week later the word appeared in Mennonite Church bulletins across Canada and the United States that

MDS was looking for three skilled workers for Skopje for a two-month period. By September 20 the three men were chosen, and on October 2 they and the three men from the Church of the Brethren left New York for their destination. Their job? To mass produce 100 prefabricated homes.

Chester Steffy wrote the first report from the volunteers: "We were stunned by the still terrible destruction evident on every hand. From a distance the large buildings don't look too bad, but on closer examination one can see they must be torn down. . . . Pray for us that the Lord's purpose for having us here will be accomplished."

One of the Brethren volunteers added: "Of course, anything can happen yet, but so far I would say that the project has been a huge success. We have real good rapport with the engineers and the architect. I feel that one can sense good or ill will in a way that transcends language barriers. In the first church service we attended we sang 'Blest Be the Tie That Binds.'"

The foreman in charge of the builders sent his congratulations on the choice of the volunteers. "They couldn't be better," he said. Relationships with national workers were excellent. The tradesmen with whom the builders worked characterized them as "friendly," "trustworthy," and "terrific."

The men seemed to want to get along with everyone, Wieler reported. "I found the Red Cross head friendly and grateful and full of praise for these Mennonites who were working so efficiently and showing their men some of the essentials of mass construction."

This official seemed genuine in his wish to bridge differences that keep nations apart. Wieler assured him that the MDS builders had come as Christians to show concern for people in need and offered additional help should another opportunity arise.

One Sunday the men went to see the graveyard where

1,500 victims of the earthquake had been buried. Photographs of the dead had been placed on many of the graves. Other graves had candles burning on them and food laid beside them. Chester Steffy wrote, "In their darkness and lack of faith they must think the departed loved ones will still know and appreciate the food and light they bring for them. If only we could help them to know the One who is the Bread of Life and the Light of the World! They told us they think the days of religion are past."

In the days before they left, the men were busy with dinner engagements. One evening they went to one of the barracks of the Serbian and Macedonian men to get a haircut. It became a friendly party. The next day they had dinner with the city government officials, several members of parliament, and the president of the Red Cross—a seven-course affair which lasted until three o'clock.

That evening the toasting continued with a party in their honor sponsored by the Red Cross. Each worker received gifts and a hearty invitation to come back, not as workmen or tourists, but as fellow Macedonians. One little delegation presented the volunteers with a box of candy and the hope it would remind them of their relationship and "that our memories like the sweets will grow sweeter each day."

Then came the final good-byes to fellow workers and the return to the United States.

Marvin Hostetler, veteran MDSer from McPherson, Kansas, speaking at a church convention in 1965, reflected on the experience of these men who worked behind the Iron Curtain:

"In my mind's eye I can see houses glistening brightly in the sunshine on the slope on the edge of Skopje. I would like to visit these homes and find out what they mean to the families living in them.

"I would be even more interested in visiting the

130

Russian soldiers who worked beside our volunteers and ate at the same table with them. What does MDS mean to them? What did Curt Regier's testimony of alternative service during World War II mean to them?

"I would like to ask the eager high school students who worked with our volunteers just what they remember about the many discussions they had with MDS volunteers. They received the tracts and listened to the stories so intently.

"How would the engineers, government officials, and those who always stood nearby just to receive a smile and handshake respond when we ask them what they remember about MDS workers?

"Our volunteers found a little Methodist church that had been deserted since the quake. They helped clear the rubble and encouraged the scattered members to begin services again. As their pastor stands before them, probably dressed in the suit left for him by Curt Regier, will the congregation remember the days when MDS men and the remaining few of their congregation joined hands and sang those wonderful old hymns in five languages, and the tears flowed down their cheeks?"

Will they remember? How could they forget?

Chapter Ten

DAY
OF DISASTER

A tragedy always happens elsewhere, to someone else. You see disasters in television suspense thrillers and in movies. You read about them in novels or in history books. In 1556, in Shensi Province, China, 830,000 persons died in an earthquake. In 1669, when Mount Etna in Sicily erupted, 60,000 people were killed. In 1887, in the Hwang River flood in China, 900,000 persons perished.

Like most people, Vera Rice of Alabama thought twisters always occurred "over there, not here."

But one day a tragedy blew "here" to Alabama. It took only two thunderous minutes. When Vera Rice and her husband, Robert, pushed open the splintered storm-cave door, all they found intact was an uncracked egg lying on the foundation where the house had stood. Five denuded chickens wandered around the debris-strewn yard in bewilderment. They had had eleven. The doghouse and the dog were also gone.

Unlike Dorothy in *The Wizard of Oz,* the Rices had no Tin Woodsman, Cowardly Lion, or Strawman to make the journey to recovery less painful. But they did receive the encouragement and support of all kinds of agencies and volunteers to rebuild and start life again. Among these volunteer agencies was Mennonite Disaster Service.

The United States and Canada faced three major

catastrophes from 1972 to 1974: (1) tropical storm Agnes that raced northward across the Atlantic States on June 23, 1972; (2) repeated Mississippi River floodings during 1973; and (3) a rash of tornadoes that hit the Middle States on April 3, 1974. Of course, this does not mean there were no localized storms and floods besides these three giants, some of them vicious and furious, but one reserves the superlatives to describe the agonies of Agnes, the incredible expanse of lands flooded by Old Man River, and the smashing violence of a hundred tornadoes.

As an opener for 1972, a 30-foot wall of water and mud cascaded through a ruptured slag dam at Buffalo Creek, West Virginia, on February 26, killing 125, destroying 450 homes, and damaging 1,600 more. It demolished fourteen communities before it emptied into the Guyana River. Because of the relative poverty of the black population and the peculiar topography of the place—a sixteen-mile long gorge in which fourteen communities nestled—the MDS recovery operation became a long-term one.

By March 10, sixty-three MDSers were at work in four areas of devastated Buffalo Creek. Through the summer they and others logged more than 4,000 volunteer days in cleanup, repairs, and other community services. In the early spring of 1973, a Voluntary Service couple moved to the area to promote a long-term MDS effort and to coordinate a summer Voluntary Service program. For MDSers, this was their first opportunity to help in West Virginia.

A second disaster in 1972 was a flashflood at Rapid City, South Dakota, on June 10. (See Chapter One.) A vicious cloudburst dumped fourteen to sixteen inches of rain in six hours and sent torrents of water crashing down the slopes of the Black Mountains west of Rapid City. Dams burst and a wall of water hit the city of 43,000 people with devastating force, leaving more than

230 persons dead and about 6,025 families victims of some damage.

MDSers from Manitoba and twelve states came quickly to the scene for the first week's mud-out and scrubdown operations. The MDSers' contribution to the summer restoration work totaled 7,000 volunteer days. A Christian contact couple moved into Rapid City for the winter to continue reconstruction and to prepare for 1973 summer Youth Flood Squads from Mennonite churches to continue in the work.

Hurricane Agnes

Even as Rapid City was digging out from its debris, Hurricane Agnes was already well on her way from her birthplace in the Caribbean. Three days after Agnes had danced the heavy fantastic up the Atlantic seaboard, Nelson Hostetter, MDS executive coordinator, issued a bulletin that "Agnes might hold the record of all time for a hurricane when we add wind, water, and flood damages. Five states—Florida, Virginia, Maryland, Pennsylvania, and New York—have already been declared federal disaster areas by the president."

On July 18, he headlined another bulletin "AGNES, QUEEN OF HURRICANES," and said, "With the exception of fatality statistics, Agnes has left a toll of confirmed figures that stretch the imagination beyond human concepts."

Hurricane Agnes thus became the first major catastrophe during the years 1972-74. On June 23, 1972, she extended her highhanded cruel reign by wind and rain over all the Eastern coastal states on that Black Friday. She danced the swollen waterways and spilled muddy floods into the basements and first floors of a hundred thousand homes, from hamlet to costly mansion.

When Agnes first approached the Eastern coast, spasmodic flooding was reported, but no one expected

Two MDSers scrub out a kitchen muddied by the 1972 flood at Buffalo Creek, West Virginia, which destroyed 450 homes and damaged 1,600 more. During the summer, MDS logged over 4,000 volunteer days in cleanup, repairs, and other community services.

permanent damage. Agnes headed out to sea, then suddenly reversed course and moved back inland. As the torrential rains continued, people struggled desperately against the rising water, setting up sandbags and bolstering dikes. Some evacuated; others ignored warnings or chose, in spite of them, to stay close to their homes.

One by one the creeks and rivers of New York, Pennsylvania, Maryland, and Virginia rolled over their banks, smashed through barriers, carried away trees, pulled down bridges, and swept into the first floor level of homes, filling them with smelly mud and muck.

From Florida to New York, Agnes left her dirty calling card. Indeed, so all-pervasive was the oozing, mildewing sediment that 1972 could be called appropriately "The Year of the Mud." The Susquehanna River came into Harrisburg and Wilkes-Barre, the Chemung River into Corning, the James into Richmond, and hundreds of swollen smaller streams into other towns and cities.

When the rains subsided and the water receded, people came out of attics and high school gyms to stare at a mud-covered, devastated land—130 persons dead, 7,000 homes gone, 161,000 families affected. At least six billion dollars' damage. "The worst in United States history!" said *U.S. News and World Report.*

Already involved in two large-scale operations in Buffalo Creek and Rapid City, MDS could have questioned its ability to cope with a catastrophe of such mind-boggling scope. Instead crews immediately spread throughout the countryside and into the cities of the states hardest hit. "God is asking us, His servants, to reach out with hands of mercy and arms of concern, motivated by hearts overflowing with compassion," said Nelson Hostetter, executive coordinator.

MDS response was as widespread as the disaster. In the first two months after Hurricane Agnes, MDS logged a total of 37,000 volunteer days in Florida, Virginia, Maryland, New York, and Pennsylvania.

In Wilkes-Barre, Pennsylvania, the city heaviest hit by Agnes, volunteers mudded out 7,000 homes in 11,000 days of free labor over a period of four months. Residents marveled at the Mennonite way of celebrating July Fourth, as hundreds of volunteers swarmed into the community to aid the holiday cleanup.

Tons of flood-ruined furnishings were hauled from homes. Women swept, shoveled, or scrubbed concrete-like mud that caked the first and second floors of many homes. Men did the heavier work, moving bedding, stoves, refrigerators, and carpeting to sidewalk curbs.

"We couldn't have done it without the Mennonites," said one resident.

At Harrisburg, within a twelve-block territory, MDSers worked in a black community; assisted with cleaning out a community drugstore; a family doctor's office; homes of elderly, retired Jewish persons; and a Lutheran church which had lost its sanctuary and first-floor furniture.

"Come to church tomorrow morning," Pastor Arthur Histand phoned his members of the Union Valley Mennonite Church, Rome, Pennsylvania, on Saturday evening."Wear boots and bring shovels." On Sunday morning his members traveled twenty miles to Athens, Pennsylvania, to help in the cleanup.

At Elmira and Corning, New York, the MDS units from Ontario and New York State went to work while their Pennsylvania brothers were involved in home communities. Later, many students joined the reconstruction work at Elmira-Corning during Thanksgiving, Christmas, and spring 1973 vacations.

Two months after Agnes swept the five-state area, disaster agency officials started preparing their reports of cleanup operations to submit to state capitals, the Office of Emergency Preparedness, and the American Red

137

Cross. MDS coordinators and directors found 37,000 MDS volunteer days had been logged during this phase of the work. Of these, 24,485 were in Pennsylvania, hardest hit by the storm, distributed as follows: 11,000 in Wilkes-Barre and the Wyoming Valley area; 6,500 at Harrisburg and other nearby towns; and the balance scattered throughout the state. Slightly more than 3,000 volunteer days were contributed in the Elmira-Corning area.

After the initial cleanup, MDS assigned a full-time social worker to investigate in depth the needs of the minimal income families and elderly. Program directors laid groundwork for long-term reconstruction and rehabilitation programs in Harrisburg, Wilkes-Barre, and Elmira-Corning.

In a year (1972) when major disasters were front-page headlines, less impressive destruction became little more than small-town news. Throughout the United States and Canada, MDS coordinated local efforts in response to such catastrophes. Flash floods struck New Braunfels, Texas, and Brainerd, Minnesota. A tornado hit Hanston, Kansas. Residents of Big Sur, California, suffered mud slides.

Heavy rains in Arizona were specially destructive to homes of Hopi Indians at Moenkop. Rain washed away much of the eighteen inches of sod used to insulate their roofs. Flooding also knocked out their open-trench irrigation system.

Rain and high winds caused Lake Erie and Lake Huron to flood surrounding communities. In Monroe, Michigan, MDSers aided 700 low-income families whose homes were damaged as a result. Eight hundred low-income families in flooded Toledo, Ohio, received MDS aid, as did flood victims in Pelee Point, Ontario. Most of these MDS efforts were short-term. MDS completed one long-term hurricane reconstruction and rehabilitation project in south Texas.

Year of the Mighty Miss

The second major catastrophe of the three-year period was the four-time overspilling and flooding of the Mississippi River during the middle half of 1973. The waters of the Mighty Mississippi inundated twelve million acres of cropland. The drowned lands on both sides of the river and its tributaries constituted a north-south corridor of disaster through the central part of the United States. The floods forced 20,000 families from their homes. Some families were washed out four times in one year. *Newsweek* (May 7, 1973) quotes historians as saying these were the worst floods in 200 years. More than 6,000 families—most of them low income, elderly, and from minority groups—needed major repairs, reconstruction, or relocation after the five-month flood. About 19,000 volunteer days were contributed.

Although the Mighty Miss played the lead role in the tragedies of 1973, storms played secondary parts in scattered tornadoes and flash floods in a dozen states: Jonesboro, Arkansas; Brent, Alabama; Asheville, North Carolina; Athens, Georgia; and Abbeyville, South Carolina. MDS volunteers gave a hand at all of these disaster sites, but the recovery programs were generally of the emergency and short-term types.

Year of the Winds

If 1972 was the Year of the Mud, then 1974 could be dubbed the Year of the Winds when 148 tornadoes hit the Middle States and South and jabbed as far north as Windsor, Ontario, on Easter weekend, April 3. The hopscotching twisters played their game of tag northward across eleven states. Worst-hit were Alabama, Tennessee, Kentucky, Indiana, and Ohio. The unbelievable winds, attaining velocities between 100 and 300 miles per hour, killed 329 men, women, and children; injured more than 4,000; and affected nearly 24,000 families. Damages exceeded $700 million.

Officially twelve hundred MDS volunteers helped clean up the gigantic mess strewn across the country. But some congregations went to work in their local areas and didn't get into the formal count. Volunteers caught chickens, cleaned streets, fitted clothing, operated chain saws, sought out the neediest people, cleaned up debris in the fields. And they listened to people talk about troubles caused by tornadoes.

Brandenberg, Kentucky, an old, quiet town of 1,800, county seat, thirty-two miles west of Louisville, was 80 percent leveled. Thirty-one people died; over 200 were injured. All was tragedy and confusion that night of the tornado. A middle-aged man walked up to one of the few buildings still standing.

"Anyone know who is in there?" he asked.

"Looking for someone?" a bystander responded.

"My wife and three kids," was his answer.

Nearly everyone was looking for someone, as rescuers pulled apart wreckage to reach survivors.

Fifty-two MDS volunteers traveled to Brandenberg by chartered bus from Kansas and Oklahoma for initial cleanup. Nineteen Amish Mennonites joined the MDS recovery operation.

At hard-hit Stamping Ground, Kentucky, Mayor Clayton Kidwell said, "One afternoon on the third day after the storm the Mennonites came in. They said, 'What can we do to help?' We had some help, but it was so unusual to have people coming from Canada and all over to help a little place like Stamping Ground. It really gave us a boost while we were down. I'm worried because I can't express our real appreciation for all the Mennonites have done, especially the coming of the young people, about forty, by chartered bus from Oklahoma under the supervision of Dean Shantz. They picked up small items like nails, which the bulldozers did not get. They worked hard."

Edward Denker, Louisville, Kentucky, whose house

140

had been severely damaged, at first planned to sell his house and buy elsewhere because his insurance didn't cover the damages. He contacted Nelson Martin, MDS coordinator, for advice. Nelson and MDS volunteers fixed the wall, roof, and porch free.

Denker said, "This experience is something. The people of Louisville couldn't believe that someone would come in and do something for you. We made a lot of good friends. . . . It's really Christianity put to practice. . . . You give them a glass of water, and they thank you for it, and here they are doing all the work for me.

"We had a little supper for them, played volleyball. We had the Catholics, the Episcopalians, the Baptists, and Mennonites and the Amish—everybody getting together! I think that's Christianity.

"Well, I know even a little donation in the basket at Christmastime makes one feel better, so you can imagine what it makes these men feel like for helping people this far away. It's a lot harder giving your time than it is to give a nickel or a dollar or ten dollars. To come all the distance from Wisconsin and Pennsylvania and Kentucky and Indiana, it's just a wonderful thing."

MDS helped him to stay. Ten of fourteen neighbors left.

Jessica Daniels, a reporter for the *Louisville Record*, a Catholic newspaper, described the coming of the MDS volunteers this way:

"Fifteen Mennonite volunteers from Pennsylvania, Maryland, and Kentucky spent last week rebuilding a tornado-ravaged home on Grinstead Drive. Ranging in age from fifteen to seventy-seven, they swarmed above, inside, and around the house like so many bees hard at work on a hive.

"Although the men represented the diverse styles and customs developed within the several branches of the Mennonite Church, they all had much in common—disciplined lives, strong reliance on the Bible, fluency in

141

Pennsylvania Dutch, and a firm commitment 'to bear one another's burdens.'

"The Mennonites' evenings have been nearly as full as their days in Louisville. They have been dinner guests in the homes of several ministers, and were treated Thursday to a covered dish supper and volleyball games at St. Leonard's Church. The men were housed at the Southern Baptist Seminary, where they sang their religious songs and conducted devotions in the chapel each morning and evening. Their morning and noon meals were provided by the Red Cross through the Baptist Seminary. Some came this week from as far away as Manitoba, Canada. One man took pictures of visitors at the reconstruction site, and there was a noticeable amount of address-swapping and invitation to 'drop by for a visit.' "

In a private letter she added, "The dedication and love for God and fellowmen witnessed by MDS is fantastic."

Reporter Ellen Schuhman of the *Louisville Times* wrote:

"Love and brotherhood—along with bricks, lumber, and hard work—are reconstructing a Crescent Hill home damaged by the April tornado. The love and brotherhood come free with the hard work being donated by the Mennonites, a religious order that believes in a simple life. Last week fourteen Mennonites came to town to work on the damaged house, and when they left Saturday, the house had a new roof, a wall had been manually pulled into place, and bricks were cleaned and neatly stacked, ready to be put in place. . . . The Mennonites aim to help the elderly, minorities, and underinsured."

German Baptists, Methodists, Presbyterians, and Baptists asked to join Mennonites in MDS operations in Xenia, Ohio, population 27,000, a city heavily damaged by the tornadoes. Workers first aided city officials in

Akron MDSers help load damaged furniture in Xenia, Ohio, following heavy tornado damage.

clearing streets, and then moved on to roof repair, hauling debris and personal belongings, and distributing food, clothing, and bedding from Red Cross centers.

Mennonite young people from West Liberty, Archbold, Plain City, and Pandora, Ohio, cleaned fields on a 200-acre farm. Others removed furniture and equipment from heavily damaged schools slated for demolition.

Both Goshen and Eastern Mennonite colleges granted special leaves for volunteering students. During Passion Week, Goshen College students provided 200 volunteer days around Atwood, Milford, Leesburg, and Kendelville, Indiana.

Recognition and commendation for services rendered have come from the president of the United States, from the governors of disaster-stricken states and state legislatures, from mayors of cities and various service organizations. At the twenty-fifth anniversary meeting of MDS in Hesston in spring of 1975, national coordinator Nelson Hostetter was presented a certificate in which the governor of Kentucky named him a "Kentucky colonel." The thanks of individuals who have been helped by MDS have been so numerous and sincere that one MDS coordinator exclaimed, "I'm scared! MDS is receiving a public image that will be hard to live up to."

"I appreciate it just an awful lot," said a resident of Forrest City, Arkansas, whose house MDS volunteers were rebuilding. "These are the finest people I've ever met." He wanted to have the MDS address to send a donation when he got back on his feet financially.

Another person who was helped said simply, "Jesus was here today."

However, the Lebanon, Pennsylvania, MDS unit declined recognition at a banquet with the words: "We should not be honored for merely performing our Christian responsibility."

Though MDSers often get pushed into the role of do-gooders, their deeper longing is that troubled, hurt individuals struggling to find a new life after the disaster may see their coming as did a Red Cross official in Hebron, Nebraska, several years ago:

"One thing that we sometimes fail to recognize is the fine Christian influence that your men have upon the people in the communities where they are assisting. In years to come, they may forget all the hard work and help you have given, but the Christian spirit that they leave with the people will continue and become a part of the lives of the families who have needed assistance."

When that happens, MDSers are content.

And Still More Disasters

The year 1974 was plagued with even more destruction. Tornadoes tore into Forrest City, Arkansas, on June 6 for a $14 million loss. Two days later on June 8, Oklahoma City, Drumright, and Tulsa, Oklahoma, as well as Emporia, Kansas, were hit. A 101-bed rest home for the aged and 150 private homes were demolished at Drumright with thirteen people killed, including five from the rest home.

At Tulsa, one hundred expensive homes were destroyed by a hopscotch twister that picked out several houses here and a dozen there, and then pounced on selected barns and other buildings as it went bouncing through the countryside. Eighteen persons died.

Damage at Oklahoma City was minimal, but at Emporia, Kansas, only two mobile homes were left standing out of two hundred, while total damage was estimated at $20 million.

Chapter Eleven

BY THE WATERS OF
MENNONITE CREEK

Through the centuries Mennonites have frequently been lauded for their zeal in spreading the gospel, integrity in their personal lives and relationships with others, and their hard work. They have been known as good farmers, good cooks, good businesspersons, good workers in all vocations. Yet Mennonites have won no Oscars for working together. Often strong individualists, with a firm belief in the right of the individual to interpret the Bible according to his conscience, they have become cautious about treading on another Mennonite's toes.

Several disasters in the last decade have pushed the Mennonites together in an unprecedented way. As they responded to the sudden massive needs of hundreds of people, they laid aside their individual differences, and found they could work together.

Operation Midnight Sun

On Afognak Island, 200 miles south of Anchorage, flows a stream named Mennonite Creek. No Mennonite explorer christened it and claimed it for the followers of Menno Simons. Rather the Indians of the area made it a permanent monument to the Mennonites who helped them following the earthquake of 1964.

The Alaska earthquake of March 27, 1964, is recorded as the most violent since the 1899 shock in the

Alaskan wilds. It shook the Anchorage area like a rat in the teeth of a terrier. It attacked with the force of 12,000 Hiroshima-size atomic explosions. It dropped buildings and pavement as much as thirty feet in downtown Anchorage. Mountains shuddered and split. Highways buckled. Pavements rippled like ocean waves. Huge slabs of concrete slid out of place. Power lines broke. Buildings that remained standing were scarred with hundreds of branching cracks. The damage totaled $750 million dollars—one hundred times what it cost the United States to buy Alaska from Russia. One hundred and fifteen people died and 4,500 were left homeless.

Elvera Voth, Kansas resident, who was in Anchorage at the time, said, "When the first tremor came, we grinned. Then the logs in the fireplace started rolling, and then we started rolling. When the debris and dust cleared, we looked toward the Four Seasons Apartment House, and between us and it was a crack in the earth twenty feet wide. A man was standing in his front door looking straight down. The front porch had been shaved off. He quite obviously didn't believe it."

Other residents couldn't believe either what they saw: flattened automobiles upended, railroad cars strewn about like empty cartons, boats tossed ashore, large canneries on the shore swept away, the jumble of buildings, boats, cars, and concrete slabs left behind.

The earthquake had produced a huge tidal wave, coming up from the ocean like a monstrous sea creature, followed by a series of shock waves. These waves sped four hundred miles down the length of the West Coast to California and outward to Hawaii. *National Geographic* described Kodiak's big wave as a "cresting, thirty-foot high wall of water that thundered up the channel, lifting 100-ton crab boats on its shoulder and flinging them like empty peanut shells over the harbor's stone jetty and sometimes two or three blocks into town."

Four successive waves of icy water hit the tiny village of Afognak, 200 miles southwest of Anchorage, where fisherman John Larsen lived. "I see something coming . . . something big! Boy, this is a big one!" he shouted frantically over the transmitter of a tiny seiner off Kodiak Island. Then the wave overtook him and silenced the transmitter forever. These waves shattered or washed away twenty-three of the thirty-eight homes on the small island of Afognak. A large community building disappeared into the waters. The land on which the village was built sank eight feet.

Army, Navy, Air Force, Coast Guard, and commercial agencies rushed tons of supplies to Alaska at once. Civil Defense set up emergency kitchens. And this biggest earthquake and biggest tidal wave brought to Alaska the largest number of skilled MDS workers that had ever traveled such a long distance in response to a major disaster. Forty volunteers came to take part in Operation Midnight Sun from ten states and four provinces and from eight different branches of the Mennonite church.*

MDS coordinators Ivan Martin, of Blue Ball, Pennsylvania, and John Garman, of Saskatoon, Saskatchewan, flew to Anchorage on April 6, ten days after the earthquake, to survey the situation. They learned that Anchorage and the immediate areas nearby were receiving prompt aid from many sources, but that the outlying communities, farther away, were being neglected. The

---

*The 40 participants of Operation Midnight Sun came from the following states and provinces: Ohio, 8; Ontario, 6; Manitoba, 4; Alberta, 4; Kansas, 4; Pennsylvania, 3; Indiana, 2; California, 2; Iowa, 2; Delaware, 1; New York, 1; Virginia, 1; Illinois, 1; and Saskatchewan, 1. Eighteen were Mennonites, 7 General Conference Mennonites, 4 Mennonite Brethren, 5 Brethren in Christ, 2 Conservative Mennonites, and one each Evangelical Mennonite Brethren, Evangelical Mennonite Church, Amish, and Church of God in Christ, Mennonite.

Federal Bureau of Indian Affairs referred the two men to officers of the Forty-ninth District of Lions International, a group that was also looking for a project.

Out of these contacts grew a cooperative project to rebuild the Indian village of Afognak where John Larsen had lived. A Memo of Understanding was drawn up by the Lions Club, MDS, and the Bureau of Indian Affairs.

The Lions Club agreed to appropriate $600,000 to supply all materials for building twenty-three houses, a tent and shelter for the volunteer craftsmen, insurance, and roundtrip transportation costs for the MDS men. Initially MDS agreed to furnish six carpenters, two plumbers, and two electricians. The Bureau of Indian Affairs agreed to supervise and coordinate the project and give medical care as needed. Three successive teams of ten men would serve for six weeks each in Operation Midnight Sun.

The new village was relocated twelve miles inland from the former site and renamed Port Lion. Work began as planned with the first team of nine men arriving on May 6, the second, also of nine men, on June 17, and the third, consisting of twenty-two men, on July 22. Many other MDSers volunteered. John Garman conducted orientation sessions in Seattle, Washington, for all three teams.

The men had come to build, so they attacked their work with vigor. By the beginning of September, when MDS officially phased out Operation Midnight Sun, seven houses had been completed; eight were roughed in and ready for roofing; thirteen had pilings, stringers, and floor joists in place; five had partial pilings; three had holes dug but no pilings; one had only land cleared; and one still needed the land cleared. Most of the houses were twenty-four by forty-four feet with three bedrooms and bath. The Bureau of Indian Affairs sent in other carpenters, who, with the Indians, finished the work.

But the men were also concerned about the spiritual needs of the Indians. In addition to working on the homes, they built a small chapel with a podium and a communion table. In the evenings after work they gathered together for MDS prayer meetings and to sing. They talked about how they could introduce Christ, in whose name they had come, to the Indians.

One Indian and his daughter took two volunteers out to an island about seven miles off shore. The Indian had shown an interest in becoming a Christian. The two men had prayed for an opportunity to talk to him alone. The trip seemed to be the answer.

They left shore on a sunny, clear day. As they neared the island, the motor gave out. About the same time, a heavy fog rolled in. The four frantically took to the oars to reach the island while they could see it. On the beach, not without anxiety, the white men surveyed the situation. On the other hand, the Indian calmly waited for either the sound of a boat or the lifting of the fog.

When they were still there eight hours later, the need for food sent the Indian hunting along the beach until he found a nest of penguin eggs. He built a fire in a sheltered area and cooked the eggs. The MDSers discovered they had not yet acquired a gourmet's palate.

As the four waited for help to come, the two white men looked for the opportunity to speak to the Indian about his inner need. Finally, they told him what Christ meant to them and expressed their concern for him. They prayed with him. At that moment they heard the roar of a motorboat in the distance. The Indian poured gasoline on the beach and lit it. The boat answered their signal and soon all four were rescued. They never had the opportunity to speak to him alone again.

Though the MDSers may never know the full impact of their living and working among the Indians, they experienced the gratefulness of these people whose homes had been destroyed by the earthquake.

On the first anniversary of the Good Friday earthquake, the Indians of the newly built city wrote an open letter:

To the members of the Mennonite Faith:
To all of you who sacrificed so that we could have a better life, we say from the bottom of our hearts "Thank you." Please accept this small donation ($70) from the people of Port Lion for use in helping others as we were helped in our time of need.

The psalmist wrote of a river "whose streams gladden the city of God, which the Most High has made his holy dwelling" (Ps. 46:4, *NEB*). In the area surrounding Mennonite Creek, MDSers hope Christ will also find a dwelling place through their brief witness.

Chapter Twelve

BETWEEN
DISASTERS

Can Mennonite Disaster Service survive without frequent major disasters to keep the interest of its members alive and growing?

No problem, say MDSers.

MDS was born and developed because of specific natural disasters such as floods, tornados, windstorms, hurricanes, earthquakes, and tidal waves. The call at midnight to the MDS volunteer to be at work at a neighboring community at 8:00 a.m. to mud out a flooded basement is not an irritation, but a joy. "Disaster brings out the best in Mennonites," one church leader commented wryly.

MDSers thoroughly enjoy the difficult work of helping in a major disaster. MDS has demonstrated in the past twenty-five years that it can handle the vicious assaults of nature directed haphazardly at any and all sections of the United States and Canada. Such natural disasters will not lessen in years to come. Like the poor, they will be with us always.

Yet between the times of wide-reaching destruction, what happens to the MDSer? How does he maintain his enthusiasm for the kind of caring MDS expects of him? Without regular involvement in disaster, does concern wither in the bright sunshine of well-being?

During the early years of MDS, interest was maintained by conducting first-aid and counseling courses for prospective volunteers. Training seminars for project directors familiarized them with procedures to be followed on project sites and with past problems. Sponsoring blood donor clinics or assisting with them is a popular activity for the volunteer-in-waiting. Some units have participated in fire-fighting and search and rescue operations, or have helped at MCC relief sales. (A single sale sometimes raises more than $100,000 for the worldwide ministries of MCC.)

But units can conduct only so many training seminars without also giving volunteers an opportunity to use their new skills at least occasionally. Year after year in boot camp becomes boring.

Soon after MDS organized, units throughout the United States and Canada realized that the definition of disaster must be enlarged to include any crisis experience, natural or man-made, which an individual or group of persons cannot handle alone. To fulfill their mandate from Christ to be burden-bearers, they must meet more than needs caused by storms, floods, and earthquakes. The emotional, social, and spiritual needs caused by oppression, misuse, and abuse of personal rights must also be met. If the stress situation was caused by human factors of neglect or violence, MDS could not turn its back. Nor did it have any clause in its unwritten contract which specified time off for vacation when the hurricane or tornado season was over.

During the early 1960s some of the most difficult man-made disasters occurred in the Deep South when about forty church buildings were burned or bombed in the state of Mississippi during the civil rights disturbances. More than 3,000 black Christians were robbed of a place to worship. Because only about ten of the forty congregations had been involved in protest actions, the burnings were not considered acts of recrimination, but attempts to terrorize the people into submission.

As the Christian's answer to hate and prejudice, Mennonite volunteers from ten states and two provinces helped rebuild five churches for blacks and two for Choctaw Indians following the large-scale bombings. In most cases the destroyed buildings belonged to small rural congregations whose members were too poor to finance a rebuilding program. Because the MDS volunteers maintained a neutral attitude toward both whites and blacks, they won the confidence of many with whom they lived and worked.

Shortly thereafter, MDS leaders were confronted by the challenge of working in the inner city. They recognized that the deteriorating and deplorable housing conditions in the ghettos were probably as responsible for the many fires and riots as outright prejudice. Working in the inner city presented a clear opportunity to prevent disaster from happening and to mend fragile black-white relations.

Landis Hershey, of Lancaster, Pennsylvania, MDS Region I director, described the homes in the inner city to fellow Christians in a talk encouraging MDS to respond to the needs of the city: "Streets look more like a junkyard than a place to drive a car. Cars without engines or wheels are sitting around. Refrigerators, washing machines, and other household items can be seen in small backyards or on broken-down back porches. Streets are poorly lighted. The houses have holes in the walls and no workable plumbing fixtures. Small stoves with smoke pipes extending out the windows provide a little heat. Steps are missing; windows are boarded shut."

Many of these houses had been built 75 to 90 years ago for the wealthy class and were still structurally sound. To demolish the buildings and build high-rise apartments was not the answer. But to repair such dilapidated homes seemed fruitless.

In St. Louis, Missouri, Jeff-Vander-Lou Corporation, a nonprofit organization which gets its name from three of the most rundown streets in a fifty-block area in the community, instituted a program by which it purchased deteriorated houses for $1,000 to $2,000. Then it offered to pay for building materials to remodel the house, to provide meals for volunteer laborers, and to supervise repairs. Because labor is an expensive item in renovating an older home, the organization hoped the volunteer labor would keep costs down to where the house could be completely restored for about $10,000. Residents of the area could purchase such homes under the Federal Housing Act loan at three percent interest over twenty-five years with monthly payments of $60. It appealed to MDS to help.

Local blacks administered all Jeff-Vander-Lou projects. MDS volunteers donated about 3,000 hours to rebuild homes as well as money for certain aspects of the project. The project demonstrated that white men can work together with blacks and under their direction. Better housing was an important aspect of the project, but the strengthening of relationships between the two races was even more important.

After the riots in April 1968 in Pittsburgh, which required the calling in of the National Guard, MDS offered its assistance to the United Black Front, considered the most powerful black organization in the city at the time. UBF aimed to unify all small organizations in the black community.

Initial contacts by MDS were discouraging. Since "helpful" organizations usually disappeared after the reporters left, Mennonites were considered only another group of promise-givers.

One of the black leaders, Robert Lavell, a Christian real estate owner, said: "There's a real feeling among militant blacks that since the black community has suffered so much from whites in the past and have been deprived of so much, whites simply have some dues to pay."

However, the two groups agreed to talk. And then one day those who had decided hope for assistance did not lie in the Christian church were ready to talk about working together. The blacks agreed to allow MDS to help but made it clear who would be in charge. In effect they said, "We do not hate you. If you respect us as human beings like yourselves, you will understand why we now have to do this our way. We cannot do it all, but we have to say how it will be done."

"But will the people of your area let us come into the city with groups of men?" asked the MDS leaders.

"If you were stopped, it would be because we said so," one of the black leaders responded. "If we invite you, the black people will let you come in and work."

MDS personnel were able to say in return, "We will help you in what we believe is God's way. We feel that God is calling us through you, and we are responding to Him through you."

So, MDS was accepted in Pittsburgh because the United Black Front had invited them. MDS workers helped in that city as they did later in many others. The blacks wanted them to teach their youth how to build, how to install plumbing, how to wire houses.

Delmar Stahly, national MDS coordinator at the time, said, "There is much to reclaim in the inner city besides houses. If we respond to their desire to learn how to handle tools, how to drive nails, more will be learned. A Christian craftsman teaches much besides his manual skill. He teaches a way of life as he goes about his tasks. This is the experience that MDS seeks in the city where God works with the material at hand, be it black or white, Christian or non-Christian."

About the same time, MDS labor assisted Ebenezer Baptist Church in Lancaster, Pennsylvania, to upgrade its substandard building to a level acceptable for the city inspectors.

Tabor Community Services, a nonprofit organization, was working closely with the Lancaster Redevelopment office to make low cost housing available to lower income families using much the same procedures as Jeff-Vander-Lou Corporation of St. Louis had done. Old houses were purchased cheaply, renovated with volunteer MDS labor, and then sold to prospective homeowners.

This "between disasters" ministry to the inner city continued with urban housing projects being started in Wichita and Kansas City, Kansas, as well as in Rochester and Philadelphia in 1972. MDS members rebuilt homes of the poor. Some Mennonite congregations cooperated to reconstruct poorly built homes. Others winterized homes for the poor and elderly. In a rural area of Kentucky, one Mennonite group rebuilt a house that had been destroyed by fire.

In the spring of 1968, a Black Mennonite church located in the ghetto area of Wichita invited MDS into their community to help in youth programs, block cleanup, and day-care nurseries. The block cleanup program was begun immediately.

MDS workers returned from the inner city invariably saying, "I am not sure what I did for those in poverty, but I do know what they did for me. If I could only give as much as I have received. God has spoken to me through this experience."

Edwin Stalter, pastor of Science Ridge Mennonite Church, Sterling, Illinois, speaking at the 1969 Region II MDS meeting, said, "Too often we have locked in our love. Somehow we Mennonite people must break open the padlocks on our love. In St. Louis, for example, love can take practical shape in wood, walls, and work. To this vision, practical, properly motivated Mennonites can respond with sensible action. When our doing validates our saying, we have begun to approach an authentic Christian life."

Since that time MDS units have continued to seek

other creative and loving ways to answer the question, "How can we be more effective in helping people who need us, regardless of race, sex, or creed?" They discovered that new immigrants to the country had special needs they could meet.

In the spring of 1963, MDS workers of Lancaster and eastern Pennsylvania made the arrival of the Old Believers at the Seabrook Farms, New Jersey, campsite more comfortable for the weary travelers from Turkey. The colorful group of 240 individuals, including 121 children under seventeen, arrived in the United States following a special appeal for political asylum to Attorney General Robert Kennedy. The Russian government was interested in having the Old Believers return to "their homeland," which they had left in 1708 for Turkey in revolt against limitations imposed upon them by Peter the Great. About one thousand had returned to Russia the year before, but two persons escaped to warn the others that the promises of land and church integrity were false.

The Tolstoy Foundation assumed complete responsibility for the entire operation. The State Department covered the costs and arranged for the immigration clearance into the United States. Attorney General Kennedy granted special asylum. The campsite was donated by Seabrook Farms and made ready by MDS.

MDS workers in British Columbia had a similar opportunity to welcome six thousand Hungarian refugees who fled the country following the invasion of Russian troops in 1956. The Canadian Red Cross was responsible for housing arrangements. Though it had the needed equipment, it lacked personnel to do the work. MDS volunteers offered to make six thousand beds in the Abbotsford Air Force Base barracks and to operate a clothing depot. Later some of the Mennonites conducted English language classes for the new immigrants.

In 1975, isolated MDS units sponsored the resettlement of Vietnamese families and individuals.

In the immediate future, MDS (Canada) faces the challenge of helping resettle Old Colony Mennonites who are returning in large numbers from Latin America to their former communities.

Another minority group which received help from MDS was the American Indians of South Dakota following the seventy-one-day occupation by Indian militants at Wounded Knee in 1972. The long siege was costly in terms of loss of human life and destruction of property. Law enforcement expenses alone were estimated at over $5.2 million.

The invitation to work in the area came from Mennonite leaders Ted Standing Elk, pastor of the Porcupine Mennonite congregation, and Earl Hedlund, pastor of the Pine Ridge Mennonite Brethren Gospel Mission. After the initial three-month reconstruction program was finished, a long-term community development effort was started.

The MDS executive committee approved funds and plans for home repairs and reconstruction of damaged and vandalized residences at Wounded Knee for three months. MDS planned to meet the needs of the Indian families who had suffered losses or damages to their homes during the period of siege. In this effort MDS cooperated with local ministerial associations, the Pine Ridge Reservation ministerial association, and the tribal and district councils.

One of the young men who spent time at Wounded Knee repairing houses damaged not during the feuding, but in disrepair because of neglect, wrote: "It is quite true that in many cases the work we did could have been done by the Indian people themselves. But it is also true that the Indians would not do such repairs . . . .

"We realized that if we were attempting to change the Indian people, we were barking up the wrong tree. We decided that probably the only results of our work was that a number of children would spend a warmer winter. . . . We found that a great deal of the benefits of our work went not to the native people, but to ourselves. To a small degree we were exposed to Indian life and culture. I definitely discovered that there are many flaws in our stereotype which portrays Indians as lazy drunkards who should be made to work. In a small way I was struck by the beauty of these people, even though I could not hope to understand their values. But we felt we were obeying Christ's commands to help those in need."

Working with native Americans has continued to be a long-term project for numerous MDS units in both the United States and Canada.

A new development in MDS work in the middle sixties was the offer of approximately one hundred fifty of the 270,000 ham radio operators in the United States at the time to serve as a communications network between a disaster area and the coordinating office. Such immediate voice-to-voice contact would save money and provide a medium for sending messages when telephone lines were down. A list of the names, addresses, and call numbers of Menno-Net was prepared for use in emergency. In 1975, the call went out to Menno-airmen to add their names to this international network of radio ham operators and airplane pilots standing by to assist in time of disaster.

Other projects to keep interest alive between disasters vary from community to community. In one city, some MDS women launched a Headstart school project, while the men refurbished an old school building for an adult educational center. Some MDS families have participated in foster child care; men have served as Big Brothers to juvenile delinquents and school dropouts or helped men newly released from jail adjust to their new environment.

In the fall of 1975 Lonnie and Jan Buerge of Elkhart,

Indiana, moved to Atlanta, Georgia, as social workers to investigate the needs of individuals and families as a result of the March tornadoes. They are the fourth team of social workers to be sent out on a special MDS assignment.

Project after project could be added to this list of what MDS volunteers do when the winds stop blowing and floodwaters recede. Frank H. Epp, presently president of Conrad Grebel College, Waterloo, Ontario, speaking at an all-unit meeting in Kitchener, Ontario, in 1965 said that in a sense MDS is simply a broadening of the concept of the service of deacons in the church. It is the Mennonite Deaconate Service of the whole Mennonite Church. It is that laymen's movement which looks after all the needs and helps in all the crises which confront Mennonites and their neighbors.

Between disasters, what does MDS do?

It continues to be the broad shoulder on which a suffering world can lean.

Chapter Thirteen

THE CHURCH
THAT GREW OUT
OF DISASTER

Each Sunday about ninety to 100 persons meet for fellowship and worship in the Masonic Hall in Big Flats, New York. The group calls itself the Community Mennonite Fellowship. It includes all sorts of people. Some have traditional Mennonite names like Bomberger, and Kolb, Buckwalter, and Herr. Others bear names like White, MacDonald, Vlasits, and Johnson.

Some grew up in the Mennonite Church; others stem from mainline denominations or have no religious background. Occupations vary from engineers to teachers and factory workers. Many are college students.

Some come with a firm commitment to a church in which the Spirit of Christ is working His will; some are still searching. All are welcome.

The group is young. It began small—with ten people meeting in the community room of a local bank in March of 1973. It celebrated its second anniversary on March 16, 1975.

The Community Mennonite Fellowship in the Corning-Elmira area of New York is a group of believers which determines to fit its faith and deeds to the needs of the people living in the community. During its brief history, it has struggled intensely to find its identity as a caring body of committed Christians whose unity is not in the religious or ethnic background or social class of its members, but in the Holy Spirit. Yet despite the pain of daily confrontation with the problems of an urban people—many of them suffering because they lack a spokesman to speak up for their needs—arising in part out of natural disaster, the church continues to grow.

In June of 1972, most of the members of this congregation didn't know the others existed. However, a unique chain of events, beginning with a hurricane, brought them together. The big events and the visible elements in this chain, which people could see and experience, like clean basements and new roofs, were chronicled in the daily newspaper at regular intervals. The miracle of how the Holy Spirit worked in the hearts of individuals, drawing them to the area to share their time, work, and love, never became a banner headline.

Greatest Natural Disaster Strikes

CORNING, N.Y., June 23, 1972—She was a nightmare, that lady named Agnes.

Her coming was heralded by torrential rains punctuated by bolts of lightning and crashes of thunder; in her wake she left death, devastation, and shattered dreams.

Residents of the Southern Tier and northern Pennsylvania can't even say she was a hurricane, for by June 23, 1972, Agnes was a "mere" tropical storm that broke every rule in the weather book and produced the greatest natural disaster in the history of the United States.

Agnes ripped into the Corning area like the atom bomb into Hiroshima. The extent of her damage is still not fully realized and yet despite the utter ruin she brought into this area, Agnes also smashed into 233 counties in a total of seven states, leaving 130 dead (18 of them here) causing $3 billion in damages and running up a higher toll in sheer destruction than the combined tally of the five worst previous natural disasters including a hurricane, two earthquakes, and a brace of flash floods. The waters she spawned drowned 5,000 square miles of land.

Almost immediately, three days later, MDS was there to help in the initial cleanup.

Want to Share Your Burden
Say Mennonite Volunteers

July 27, 1972—"We may be strangers to you, but you are our neighbors. We cannot fully understand your loss, but we want to share your burden."

This is the thought behind the Mennonite Disaster Service. Currently there are 200 Mennonite volunteers working in the Corning, Painted Post, and Gang Mills area. They have been here since June 26 and have refurbished 24 homes in Corning and 70 in Gang Mills.

The volunteers came from various sections of Ontario, New York, Pennsylvania, and Maryland. Merle Herr, pastor of the Pleasant Valley Mennonite Church near Hammondsport, who was in charge of coordinating MDS volunteers, promised MDS would stay until Labor Day, "at least." That date was extended almost immediately.

Mennonites Seek Disaster Aides

August 1972—Mennonite Disaster Service will need volunteers for the next two years to help rebuild after the damage of Hurricane Agnes.

So estimates the MDS executive coordinator, Nelson Hostetter of Akron, Pennsylvania. Carpenters, plumbers, electricians, and masons are needed, and just plain laborers for general cleaning, said Robert Stoltzfus of Aurora, MDA coordinator for northeastern Ohio.

The call for volunteers did not go unheeded. MDS

volunteers began pouring into the community in shifts and droves.

Mennonites Spent Thanksgiving Here

November 1972—Once again the people of Gang Mills, Painted Post, and Corning areas were fortunate enough to have a large number of Mennonites helping in the area.

Over the Thanksgiving weekend a total of 67 members of the Mennonite Church donated their time and skills to area flood victims. . . . The volunteers donated a total of 536 man-hours and traveled from as far away as Indiana, Illinois, Pennsylvania, and northern New York.

On December 1, 1972, J. Merle Herr, pastor of the Pleasant Valley Mennonite Church for 3½ years and the MDS coordinator following the flood, was named director of Mennonite Ministries and of MDS's long-term projects for the area. The appointment was announced by the New York State Fellowship of the Mennonite Church and the Eastern Mennonite Board of Missions. An office was set up at Faith Baptist Church, Gang Mills.

Herr said MDS would continue flood recovery programs and begin development of related projects, such as supervising inmates of the Elmira Reformatory in a work-release program to rebuild flood-damaged homes while learning construction skills. He also envisioned introducing recreational activity into the area for the elderly and supplementing the food assistance programs to elderly and low-income families. Two coffeehouses with a resident couple in each to dialogue with students of the area were projected.

Obviously, MDS was going to stick around for a while, but the image was changing. Throughout the fall months, Mennonites from various points continued to come for shorter and longer periods of time to help with cleanup and rebuilding.

Students Join Adults in Flood Work

December 1972—A group of students and adults from widely separated parts of the country are spending this week helping area flood victims repair their homes. The project was coordinated by the Mennonite Disaster Service. . . .

A group of nearly 60 persons—half high school and college students and half adults—arrived here Tuesday and Wednesday to begin the home repair project, according to Donald Siegrist, of Jasper, an MDS spokesman.

Internationals Come
To Work with MDS

Fall 1972—In the past six months Mennonite volunteers have streamed into this area from all over North America including several states and Canada.

As of last week the volunteers have come from three continents. An African and an Indian electrical technician are working in this area in conjunction with a training program sponsored by the Mennonite Central Committee.

By the middle of the first winter following the flood, the plan that MDS volunteers would remain for two years was again revised to "as long as the need exists."

Mennonites Continue to Aid Area,
To Stay as Long as Need Exists

December 1972—Many volunteers came to this area from many places and returned to their homes since the flood of June 23, but the Mennonite Disaster Service is still in operation following its practice of helping neighbors.

Pastor J. Merle Herr . . . said that the Mennonites will serve the people all winter and possibly into next summer or as long as the need exists.

That week the general public was invited to a program presented by a group of Mennonites from

166

Grantsville, Maryland, at the Faith Baptist Church in Gang Mills. Irvin Hershberger, pastor of the Grantsville Mennonite Church, spoke on "Who Are the Mennonites and Why Do They Come to a Disaster Area?" At the end of the service, those present were given the opportunity to ask questions about Mennonites.

By December Mennonite volunteers from Maryland, Pennsylvania, New York, Indiana, Michigan, and Canada had provided 9,600 hours of labor to the people in the Corning-Painted Post area. Four hundred volunteer days of cleanup and light repair had been donated immediately after the water subsided and 800 volunteer days of skilled labor after July. MDS had helped clean up 200 homes and repair 110 residences, including restoring cellar walls and major carpentry projects. In the Elmira area, MDS had provided help in 1,500 homes, amounting to 2,000 volunteer days.

Gifts from the community made it possible for MDS to continue the repair work and to buy building supplies. Rotary International District 712 Food Relief Fund donated $4,500. Additional money came from other sources.

Area residents tried to express their appreciation for the work the Mennonites were doing. Richard C. Loll, mayor of the city of Elmira, New York, issued a special proclamation of thanks to the city of Elmira, Ontario, for the help it had received from the twin city.

Area reader opinion columns carried letters like these:

> There is no money in the world that could be paid to them [MDS] for the dirty work they did. They should be paid. They cleaned out a flooded rental property . . . for us. The house had roaches, fleas, and possibly bedbugs, not left by the flood but by the tenants who now moved into HUD trailers. The tenants didn't clean it or ever try to. The Mennonites saved us a citation from the Board of Health.

* * *

Both my husband and myself are retired on total disability. We can do absolutely nothing, and I can do some light work. We lost everything in the flood, but the house was left in very poor condition.

Right after the flood we had many youngsters, Mennonites and other people, clean up the yard. This we could not do. . . . They deserve so much credit that words do not express what the younger generation is doing for the community. All I can say is, "Thank God for the youngsters of today."

In the spring of 1973, the Jaycees of the Elmira-Corning area chose the Mennonites to receive the 1972 Distinguished Service Award. Specifically, the award went to Pastor J. Merle Herr, director of Mennonite Ministries in Elmira and Corning.

Herr, sensing that some of the community citizens saw the Mennonites as unusual people "who have come here to do some spectacular things that set Mennonites apart from being something more than the average person," wrote an open letter that was published in area newspapers. "As Mennonites," he wrote, "we readily acknowledge that we are people with the same struggles, same frustrations, same temptations and desires as anyone else; thus we suffer from the same failures, mistakes, and sins as anyone else." He hoped that people would see the MDS volunteers as Christians "serving in the name of Christ and not as Mennonites here to claim any credit to ourselves."

In the winter of 1972-73, one editor told his readers the next phase of the MDS ministry.

Flood's Gone, But Not Mennonites

CORNING, N.Y.—The hardy Mennonite Disaster Service (MDS) is digging in for the winter.

The volunteers who help with flood recovery will keep coming into the Corning-Elmira area through the end of summer, said Pastor J. Merle Herr, director of Mennonite Ministries in Corning and Elmira.

What's more, MDS has plans to set up permanent offices, centers for continuing Mennonite Ministries in Corning and Elmira.

In January of 1973, MDS acquired a flood-damaged house at 269 West Pulteney Street in Corning. After volunteers had renovated it, it would become the permanent headquarters of MDS.

Herr told reporters, "We really have a much broader concern in this area than just flood repair. We are sensitive to social problems. If we see a special problem, we try to become involved as quickly as possible." He cited work among the youth, the aged, and those in prison as areas of immediate concern.

The same month Ken Zehr, of Bath, joined the MDS staff as its first full-time social worker for a one-year term. One of Zehr's responsibilities was to act as a counselor to and spokesman for flood victims. Many persons were not receiving adequate financial aid because they did not know which agency provided which funding. Zehr acted as their advocate. Often following a disaster, a victim's spirits remain low and depressed. Zehr gave support by listening and offering advice.

That spring the nucleus of Christians was enlarged when several families, living in different parts of the country, each unknown to the others, were led of God to move to the Corning-Elmira area to work for MDS in repair and reconstruction and to begin building the Church of Jesus Christ which is not made of stone or bricks.

Daniel Buckwalter, who was appointed MDS project foreman, and his wife, Helen, moved to a trailer near the MDS center from Troupsburg, New York, forty-five miles away.

Joe and Lorraine Kolb, formerly of Wellsboro, Pennsylvania, also moved into a trailer in the area. Joe, a carpenter, gave up his own business to work with

MDS. Lorraine, a home economics teacher who formerly directed a day-care center, anticipated the possibility of counseling in family living.

The other families included Richard and Deborah Buckwalter, Parkesburg, Pennsylvania; Willie Hurst; the Galen Lehmans of Chambersburg, Pennsylvania; and the Stan Mitts from Ontario, Canada. Hurst was a carpenter, Lehman an electrician, and Mitts a sign painter interested in reformatory work in Elmira.

The group grew again when Voluntary Service youth, sponsored by Mennonite Central Committee, arranged to come in units of ten persons to work for ten weeks. They were housed and fed in the renovated Pulteney Street headquarters.

These families, the Herrs, the VSers and a few interested community people were the cluster of Christians of like faith and vision who thought about becoming an organized church. Several families in the community indicated interest in participating in small Bible studies.

In addition to this permanent group of workers, volunteers continued to come from outlying areas. The weekend of February 10, 1973, fifty-nine volunteers arrived from New York and Pennsylvania and worked in thirteen homes. During January, a group of college students had come from Bethel College, a Mennonite-affiliated college in North Newton, Kansas, to assist in counseling and other work. At the end of the first semester, a group of nine students from Conrad Grebel College, Waterloo, Ontario, took ten days between the end of their school term and the beginning of summer school or summer jobs to assist persons hit by the flood.

Herr said, "We're seeing over and over in MDS that young people are responding and finding meaningful experiences by giving of themselves to help others who have need."

One young person told him, "This has brought us

MDSer Cindy Miller helps construct a house in Elmira, New York, damaged by Hurricane Agnes.

together and made us part of the church."

As in other MDS projects, MDS efforts were chan-
neled to persons who needed help because they could not
help themselves.

In early summer of 1973, the plans that MDS would
remain in the area first for six weeks, then for two years,
then as long as the need existed, were changed again.
Herr told the community the Mennonites weren't planning to get out—ever.

Mennonites Here to Stay

June 10, 1973—"We've been to a lot of places—but
this area stands out as a place that has really been
responsive to our efforts."

With that comment, Pastor J. Merle Herr, director
of the Mennonite Ministries for Corning and Elmira,
announced that Mennonite centers are being established in the two cities on a permanent basis.

First, the Mennonites came last year to help dig
slime and mud from flood homes. Then, they
returned to help with repair work. Now they have decided to stay.

The Elmira city council responded to the statement by
passing a resolution officially welcoming the Mennonites to the community.

For the summer of 1973 a home repair program was
projected in cooperation with the Corning Glass Works
Foundation. Earlier plans to begin a coffeehouse and
youth ministry and to become involved in prison work
were being developed. A year-round social work
program was projected. Mr. and Mrs. Richard
Buckwalter were appointed directors of the Corning office and Mr. and Mrs. Joseph Kolb of the Elmira center.

By the fall of 1973, the number of Mennonite families
who had "set their faces toward new land"—Corning
and Elmira, N.Y., and who, unlike most MDS workers,
did not plan to return home after several days, weeks, or

months numbered eleven. This group included two carpenters, two electricians, several cooks, a mason and plumber, a secretary, and several people interested in informal counseling.

"There were no Mennonite people or programs in Corning or Elmira before Hurricane Agnes hit in 1972," Herr told the press. "We had felt for several years that something ought to be happening here. The flood brought us."

The group, now considerably larger, worshiped together every Sunday. On Tuesday evening the Corning Mennonites gathered and on Wednesday the Elmira group met for sharing and prayer. Their goal was not to fill up a large church building with 100 people in six months. "Our concern is to become caring persons in the community," said Herr.

By April of 1974, Herr could announce the next step in this program of caring in the Corning-Elmira area— the Menno Housing Project. Many of the homes flooded in 1972 had been repaired to a better condition than before the flood, thereby increasing the rent and making it impossible for families with fixed incomes to return to them.

Under this new project, Mennonite Ministries planned to purchase 20 vacant lots and flooded homes and either build new homes or rebuild damaged homes, and then offer them for sale at about $15,000 to families who could not afford a home of their own or who did not have the funds for a down payment. This low price was possible because labor for building these homes would be donated by volunteer craftsmen and work-release prisoners.

MDS planned to draw on established community resources, such as the Family Service Society, the county Social Services Department, and local ministers for solutions to problems in connection with this project that would require outside help. In addition, counselors associated with MDS would offer assistance with family budgeting, job hunting, homemaking, family conflicts, and social adjustments.

For this ambitious project, MDS had planned no formal fund drive, but in time approached industry, churches, civic organizations, and others. Their operational budget was $380,000, including $30,000 committed to the project by MDS. Other projected income included pledges from local churches, $10,000; United Way, $10,000; civic organizations, $5,000; regional diocese, presbyteries, and organizations, $25,000; and corporate foundation funds, $300,000.

The $300,000 was to become a revolving account, to be used to start construction, then used again as mortgages were obtained and the money was returned. The project was not to be a giveaway, but the means of helping families who had lost their homes become independent members of society. In moving into this area of work, MDS knew that other agencies such as Elmira Aid, Inc., and the Office of Human Development were already involved, but there was more work than these groups could handle.

By November of 1974, four homes, twenty-four by forty feet with full basements and three bedrooms, were under construction in Corning and Gang Mills. Plans were to construct several more during the winter. An assessment of the situation showed that over 200 housing units were needed for the elderly, 45 percent of whom had annual incomes of less than $7,000; 800 family units with two or three bedrooms were needed, of which 75 percent of the families had annual incomes of less than $7,000.

In order to be alert to community needs and feelings, a committee of responsible persons representing the various interests of the area was invited to meet regularly to evaluate the program and become the liaison between MDS staff and community.

In the meantime the group of Christians which had begun meeting in the bank building had moved into the living room of the Corning Center and then to the Masonic Hall in Big Flats for worship services. During the week they carried on their work of compassion to meet the needs of the community. Work continued with repairs and construction under the housing project. Voluntary Service workers hung doors, laid blocks, and handled plumbing tools and painting projects. They worked side by side with work-release prisoners from the New York State Reformatory at Elmira and assisted in volunteer hospital work and in the Corning Coffee House. The girls visited the elderly widowed women and sponsored teas for them every few months to bring them together in a social setting.

A top priority was learning to know and relate to the people of the community in a personal way. Three Bible study groups were opened in homes of persons not interested or ready for membership in the organized fellowship. Saturday night youth meetings brought out community college students. An active program of inviting neighbor families into homes for supper and get-acquainted times was begun. In each case the goal was to direct the people to the supreme example of love, Jesus Christ, who gave His life for the redemption of humankind.

This group of believers, bonded together by their unique pilgrimage, which included sloshing through mud, clambering on roofs, chatting over a cup of coffee, listening to stories of heartache and disillusionment, praying with one another for strength to meet the problems of the day, found they had few patterns in present-day churches to direct their growth and organization.

Together they confronted some of the hard questions which face a growing body of Christians: What are the characteristics of the ideal New Testament church which is guided by the Holy Spirit? How do the charis-

175

matic gifts operate in the church in the 1970s? How should a frontline mission, such as this group with its members from many backgrounds, relate to the organized Mennonite Church? What type of covenant should bind the members to God and to each other?

As they worked and prayed and shared together, they realized that there is no way human wisdom and ingenuity can resolve the struggles of church building in the city in this age. Christ Himself must be the Builder. Herr stated, "Lessons learned include the understanding that we cannot hurry or push for quick, easy answers or agreement on these important concerns of a new brotherhood. There were times when it became painfully obvious that the broader church did not fully appreciate the depth and/or the seriousness with which the emerging fellowship struggled with these issues."

On June 2, 1974, Community Mennonite Fellowship had the joy and privilege of baptizing twenty-two persons. On the same day it celebrated its second anniversary. Merle Herr, who had coordinated the MDS program for two years, was voted to shepherd the newly formed flock. For some time his role had already been slowly changing from primary involvement in MDS, Mennonite Ministries, and Menno Housing Project to leadership of the church. On September 14, 1975, the church baptized another fifteen persons, eleven of them adults, four teenagers.

John R. Martin, professor of New Testament and evangelism at Eastern Mennonite College, who made a two-week study of the church fellowship, said at the end of his visit: "God has done a new thing at Corning-Elmira. The development of a new unique Mennonite image by MDS, Menno Housing, and Voluntary Service, and the emergence of a Christian fellowship out of these ministries is a modern miracle."

Community Mennonite Fellowship proved that the road to Jericho for modern-day Samaritans is not always a rural path, but can sometimes be a market street, or a highway next to the cloverleaf, an industrial complex, or the suburbs of a large city.

What lies ahead? "With a look into the future we see the realistic possibility of a congregation continuing to acknowledge the claim of Christ in their day-to-day experiences, also a growing commitment to be used of the Spirit to minister to the needs of the whole person, both within the fellowship and in our communities," said Herr.

The story of Community Mennonite Fellowship has just begun.

Chapter Fourteen

REUNION TIME FOR MODERN-DAY SAMARITANS

Take a Wesleyan camp meeting. An annual church conference. A Christian workers' retreat. A family reunion. A business meeting. Mix them all together for two days and you've got the annual MDS meeting held the second Friday and Saturday in February and rotated geographically to the various regions and units.

Elemental. Celebrative. Loving. Accepting. Eager. Spirit-filled. Unsophisticated. Koinonia. Charismatic. These words attempt to describe the annual coming together of modern-day Samaritans, but even they don't do it adequately. MDS annual meeting is that and more.

MDSers wouldn't miss annual meeting for anything. One pastor resigned a church board position so he could attend. Another layman said he'd rather miss his church conference convention than the annual meeting.

At the twenty-fifth anniversary celebration of MDS in Hesston, Kansas, in February 1975, three public sessions averaged about 600 attendants. The annual fellowship banquet seated about 1,200 enthusiastic MDSers from California to New York, Oregon to Florida in the United States, and from British Columbia to Ontario in Canada.

Annual meeting is a "come as you are" festival. No one is overly concerned about length and style of hair, whether it is short, long, curly, straight, brush cut, or shag, sporting chin whiskers or sideburns. No one cares whether those present wear loud double-knit sports suits or barn-door pants and blue jeans, slacks or a dress, plain clothes or a business suit. The Amish and plain-suited Mennonites may be more generously represented at some meetings, but the mix doesn't matter. All are welcome.

MDSers come to listen and also to share their own experiences, to meet old friends and to make new ones. There's a lot of handshaking accompanied by "Say, didn't I meet you at . . . ?" Sometimes the meeting becomes one long string of joyous testimonies with people pushing to get to the microphone. The talks are spontaneous, sometimes spoken in colloquial syntax. They have no alliterative three points, so dearly beloved of preachers, no carefully polished illustrations or choice one-liners. The MDSers just tell what happened.

A natural humor, born out of the incongruities when mud, tragedy, and love are mixed in giant proportions, rises easily to the surface. It is important to tell all, the good experiences as well as the uncomfortable ones, to ask questions and to share doubts. Together MDSers relive the experiences of the past year without the smells, the heavy, muddy boots and aching muscles. They encourage each other to keep working.

What do they talk about? Some are bursting to let the others know that telling people the good news of Jesus Christ is much easier when mixed with shovels, hammers, and hoses. It's a natural.

One volunteer said, "We usually are somewhat ashamed of Jesus, but now when we serve in love, we gladly talk of Jesus. When people say, for instance, 'There must be something in you that makes you come such a long distance to help us, it is easy to answer. There is no secret about it. We love Jesus Christ and we are trying to live as we believe He wants us to live. That is it!'"

Another volunteer related the story of a woman

trapped in her home in a flood with no way out. As the waters grew higher, she moved onto a table. With only a foot of breathing space between the rising water and ceiling, she thought her time to die had come. But the waters receded and she was rescued. She questioned MDS volunteers, "Why was I spared? Was it to tell me something? Is it the message that Christ died for my sins?"

One volunteer joyfully told the others how the girl she had been working with was deeply concerned about her spiritual condition. As they worked together, the girl couldn't continue until she had made a new start with Christ. Now she was making big strides in the faith.

MDS testimonies have a quality of immediacy. Workers don't seem to agonize over the rationale for their actions; they just act—impulsively, instinctively, almost against reason. They do not ask "What does mankind need?" but the ancient question of the Prophet Micah, "What does the Lord require of me?" Their service is a free act, not forced or calculated. And if they serve in one disaster, it seems natural to volunteer for another.

After the tornado of April 3, 1974, several representatives from northern Indiana came to Louisville, Kentucky, to consider the possibility of MDS becoming involved in a long-term effort of rebuilding. Since J. Nelson Martin was the only one in their group in construction work, they asked him to help for six weeks if he could get a leave of absence from his job as mason foreman. His employer, a Christian, agreed to the six weeks. Nelson became MDS coordinator of the Louisville project.

At the end of that time, because the work was not finished, Nelson asked for another leave. He got it. Following that term, he asked for another extension. "Haven't you done your share?" people asked him. He was away from his job for a whole year, during which

Twenty-three students from Goshen College, Goshen, Indiana, led by Professor Roman Gingerich, engaged in a four-day cleanup at Hanover College, Hanover, Indiana, following a tornado in 1974.

time he lost some of his fringe benefits, such as profit sharing and insurance coverage. But he shared with the MDSers at one annual meeting other benefits which were more important to him.

"I'm just thankful for the way the Lord has led. I've been able to see His blessing on the work, confirming that this was His will for me. One time, we had about 8,000 bricks to lay for a home. We needed scaffolding and boards, and I had to make arrangements for six scaffold jacks. I knew this would not be enough, for we needed about thirty. I called a lumber company to locate materials for scaffolding, but it seemed like everything was too expensive. I prayed about it.

"Soon after this, as I was being interviewed by a reporter from the *Louisville Times,* a gentleman in a pickup truck drove up. He asked who was in charge and if we had started the brickwork yet. I explained that we were all volunteers and that we needed scaffolding and boards to begin work.

" 'I have a whole truckload of materials,' he said. 'I just finished a job and need some place to store them.' About a half hour later he pulled in with a big truck, unloaded about fifty scaffold boards, thirty-five jacks and even a mortar mixer.

"It was just really unbelievable. I just thanked the Lord for providing that need. The man was not a professing Christian, and I was able to share a little bit with him. I trust the Lord will bless him, even as he shared what he could with us."

In two weeks the man picked up his materials and would accept no pay.

Nelson's story has its counterparts in the experiences of other MDSers in many parts of the United States and Canada. Their stories of how god led them, answered prayers, restored faith, and how decisions for Christ were made sound almost like a high-powered evangelism workshop, but without the planning sessions, the brochures, the filmstrips and other paraphernalia aimed to stimulate sharing. Here it breaks forth naturally, effortlessly.

Some MDSers admit to having been a little bit ashamed about being one of those "queer Mennonites" until they find others put them on a pedestal.

At one disaster site, there were rumblings as people stood in long lines for clothing, for food, for information about housing, for word on the whereabouts of friends, for everything. Weary and frustrated, some of the individuals started to quarrel and argue. A Red Cross official came to Eddie Bearinger, MDS coordinator from Ontario, with the words: "MDS has to police those lines."

"You've got the National Guard. Why don't you use them?" replied the surprised Eddie.

"That won't work. Things will explode. You only need to send two fellows. Have them wear your insignia and talk to the people in the line."

Two men were appointed to move among the people, and emotions calmed down.

Said Big Eddie later, "That Red Cross official's confidence in the Mennonite peace witness was a lot stronger than mine. I was ashamed."

One MDS volunteer didn't know quite how to respond when someone said to him, "I understand you people are honest. We can leave things lying around." Or another, when a seventy-eight-year-old tobacco-chewing widow threw her arms around him and said, "You are the answer to my prayers." Or another, when a volunteer from another denomination commented, "We are too proud in our church to do such a job. It wouldn't go across in our churches."

The whole audience at the annual meeting rejoices with the volunteer who tells how his spirits were lifted when he saw how one family met disaster with faith and courage. He was working in a tornado area in which a family told him that they had been away for Sunday dinner with friends when the storm came smashing through the community. It swept their property so clean that the only thing left beside the concrete foundation was an old metal water tank.

They told the MDSer: "You know we actually are at the place where we value this experience. We have never known human love, we have never known human relationships, we have never known our neighbors and even friends from far away like we know them now. We wouldn't miss this experience. It's been one of the richest times of our lives."

For some volunteers helping at a disaster site and confronting the ugly wound of deep emotional hurt is a painful experience. When visions and dreams for the future are buried in six inches of mud, they learn that flippant answers such as, "Everything will turn out fine," are empty phrases. They feel compelled to share with others at the annual meeting their gut-level feeling of awe at the size of the force which caused so much wreckage and of their own puniness when they realize they are expected to help.

One volunteer at Wilkes-Barre, Pennsylvania, said: "I thank God for this kind of experience with young people. I came to Wilkes-Barre. I was scared. I had so little orientation. The need was so vast. We parked our camper on the lawn of a church. The pastor was often in tears. One of the things I had to learn was how to accept the thanks that poured in."

Another said, "I shall never forget one of the first sights I saw—mud being shoveled out of windows on the first floor, the second floor, the third floor. Amid all the rubble and ruin we saw faces—empty faces, dazed faces, hopeless faces."

Still another said: "We came to a beautiful house, and there was a lady just standing there paralyzed by all the work to be done. But you should have seen the change in her when just a few persons came to help."

Some volunteers were visiting with a couple who were surveying the damage to their home. It seemed a total loss. As they tried to express their concern, the man said, "This is nothing. I have been through hell." He had spent five years in a concentration camp. What does one say then?

One volunteer reported he had been with a farmer, surveying the damage from heavy wind. The man had cows to milk, but no barn. That afternoon the insurance agent had notified him that because of a foul-up in communications his policy had lapsed. He seemed calm in spite of it all. As they walked by the shed and saw a new car about a week old supporting the side and roof of the barn, the man broke into tears. The new Ford was not his most prized possession; it was just the straw which broke the camel's back. Being close to people pushed to the limits of their strength by calamity removes all flippancy and cocksure responses. At such times MDSers report the best response is to be silent and listen, sympathetically.

At the annual meeting, volunteers share their experiences, but those who have been helped come long distances to tell their side of the MDS story as well.

Roger Newell, former Methodist minister and director of a newly organized disaster program in Kentucky told the 1975 meeting about the changes in his life since his experience with MDS.

"Our church had never taken in strangers," he said. "MDS opened the town. It opened a new opportunity for me in the State Interchurch Recovery Program. It has led me into the halls of the Kentucky capitol to give witness to politicians. You've taught me a lot about life and the Lord. The reason God has honored you is because you live your faith, not talk it. No man can ever meet a Mennonite and be the same. My life has changed for the best because it's been for God."

He had brought along a young girl, Lavina Fadenrecht, who told the audience how she had accepted Christ because of the MDS witness.

Rosemary Paris, Xenia, Ohio, was one whose house and business was rebuilt by MDS. She told the 1975 annual meeting that she had owned and operated a day-care center before Xenia had blown away. The house was leveled except for the basement. For almost four days the family lived without heat, water, and food.

"I didn't know anything about the Mennonites but saw people cleaning, building, and moving wall partitions in the neighborhood." She went to a Mennonite named Eli who told her he had been praying for someone of her race to ask for help.

"Well, here I am," she responded. She bought building materials which the Mennonites used to rebuild her house. "The people of Xenia thank God for the Mennonites," she concluded.

After hearing such words of praise and recognition, the MDSers admonish one another to push the halo down over their heads and keep working. "Before our heads swell too much, let's realize we are doing all of this in the name of Christ." Too much praise and glory almost embarrasses them.

At the annual meeting you hear little talk about some of the questions which bother some individuals such as inter-Mennonite and interchurch cooperation. Ecumenicity is implicit, accepted, and cherished in MDS. It belongs. MDS couldn't function any other way. Testimony after testimony mentions how good it is to work together with other Mennonites and other denominations. This free-form ecumenicity is an enlarging experience for them, especially when they hear people of other faiths they've been conditioned to think of outside the fold speak the same evangelical language as they do. They discover God calls them to openness of mind and heart.

Though at every level of organization in Christendom at large, churches and Christians are divided among and within themselves over which of humankind's needs should have first claim on finances and personal resources, MDSers seem to have been able to integrate evangelism, missions, and social action into one unified whole. Subconsciously they know they are not just the "overalls" department of the church. Their work is faith as much as anything else which is done in loyalty to Jesus Christ. And they think it is important to keep telling each other this.

Through the testimonies, panel discussions, and talks, one senses a probing for better answers to meeting the needs of disaster victims. The usually excellent turnout of volunteers in response to a coordinator's appeal for help doesn't always show all sides of the picture. Sometimes the coordinator needs to make seemingly endless phone calls for volunteers. What he thought of as an inexhaustible supply of help has dried up. He can hardly face his phone. He asks the group what he should do.

Discussion focuses on other matters that concern everyone. What should MDS do about follow-up of persons who have made meaningful commitments to Christ? Should MDS try to arrange for worship and fellowship opportunities for these people?

One person is troubled about knowing how well he has shared the faith and gotten across reasons for service. Do people actually see MDSers as committed followers of Christ or merely as do-gooders?

Some volunteers sense the need for more training in helping in a disaster, not only in cleanup, but in counseling and sharing their faith. Where can they get such help?

Other questions which have to do with long-reaching policies crop up also. Should MDS accept donations from civic and government agencies which might bind them?

Should MDS remain an "in-and-out" kind of ministry or continue to move into more long-term projects? Yet in staying so long in one project, is MDS using up people-power which would not be available in case of another emergency?

What should be the relationship of MDS to injustices and inequities that occur on a disaster scene when the wealthy are often the first and largest recipients of aid while poor people are pushed back?

How can MDS avoid leaving the impression that they are giving only free labor, free repairs, free service—and make clear that their motivation is to serve in the name of Christ?

The tough questions don't frighten MDSers into quitting. Even though some questions have no immediate answers, the volunteers are ready to keep working on them during the coming year. MDS's annual meeting has served as sort of clearinghouse. It's as if the umpire has announced once again, "No hits, no runs, no errors. Player up to bat." And in this case, MDS is ready to go to bat once again for people thrown a vicious curve by disaster.

One observer at an MDS annual meeting commented: "This layman's movement is the most exciting development in the Mennonite Church in recent years. Individuals eager for fellowship and opportunities for humanitarian service have found a meaningful way to express their needs in a church-related way. They no longer feel like helpless particles in a conglomeration of humankind, but purposeful helpers. They think it is great."

Another observer added: "I had a clean, washed feeling after attending the MDS meeting. MDS is like a third force in Mennonitism which intellectual theologians and church bureaucrats have scarcely recognized . . . it's all a bit scary; MDS is like a church without the structure of a church."

Does that really matter?

APPENDIX A

Humor in Overalls

The prisoners from a local penitentiary were assigned to the MDS director as "volunteers" in a "work release program" to assist in flood recovery work. After several days of working with the MDS volunteers, one of the prisoners said to the coordinator, "Eddie, you've shown us a lot of work. Now what about the release?"

* * *

Noah Kolb, MDS emergency project director at Wilkes-Barre, Pennsylvania, floods, likes to be introduced as a relative of the earliest man in the flood business—the one who built the ark.

* * *

Ray Hess of Souderton, Pennsylvania, enjoys talking about the Wilkes-Barre flood, but he fears when he gets to heaven he'll be upstaged by another man who has bigger and better flood stories to tell when the water stood around for forty days, not just forty hours.

* * *

A Red Cross executive came to an MDS coordinator and said, "My rabbi tells me you cleaned his house and found his wife's ring in the mud. I'm an honorary rabbi. I'd like to be an honorary Mennonite." So the MDS man pinned an MDS badge on him.

* * *

After the Buffalo Creek operations, MDS headquarters received a contribution from the communities where West Virginia victims had been assisted. The letter was sent to "Men in Night" Disaster Service.

* * *

At Tulsa, someone nailed a sign to a house that had its front side blown away. The sign read, "Open House."

* * *

Some volunteers found this wall motto while rummaging in the debris of a souvenir shop: "God Bless This Mess."

* * *

A Roman Catholic priest offered to host a Mennonite Disaster Service team while they worked in the area. He expected two or three persons. "The Lord blessed us a hundred-fold," he said. His request: a Mennonite cookbook for Catholic rectories.

* * *

One pastor received a call from a member inquiring whether it would be all right if the congregation suspended church services on Sunday to help flood victims clean their houses. The pastor gave his okay.

"If the pastor thinks it's okay, then we think it's okay," said the church member. That Sunday the congregation met in house churches—with their feet ankle-deep in mud.

* * *

Some youngsters in Rapid City turned in 76 cents of their earnings from a lemonade stand. "We wanted to give this for MDS," they said. Added to the note were the names of the children and the line, "Jamie Smith helped too."

* * *

And other signs:
"House for Sale with Indoor Swimming Pool"
"Spring Cleaning—We Haven't Cleaned So Well in Years"
"House for Sale: Recently Remodeled by Mr. Susquehanna"
Newspaper headline: "Amish Came from Paradise to Muck of Harrisburg."

* * *

Sayings born from a mixture of mud, muck, and love:
He who moves mud finds a friend.
We are here to be forgettable, so Christ is memorable.
You can't just be a good egg. You either have to hatch or go rotten.

What one treasured yesterday is but trash today. Flood is no respecter of persons.

A flood is a river that grew too big for its bridges.

* * *

A flood victim, whose house was knocked off its foundation and was sitting at an odd angle, posted the sign for tourist photographers: "If it's worth a shot, it's worth a buck." A collection container stood beneath the sign.

* * *

One Mennonite who knew nothing about MDS discovered it through his governor. A tornado hit Hanston, Kansas, damaging the farm of a Mennonite businessman. His fences disappeared and scattered the stock over the countryside. So he phoned the governor of Kansas asking for help from the National Guard to gather his livestock. The governor replied: "Until the red tape is cut in getting the National Guard out for a case like yours, the Mennonites could have it all cleaned up."

* * *

A group of volunteers had worked particularly hard helping a woman clean up her house after the flood. They mucked and mudded. They thought they had done a good job. Next day they received a phone call from her. Could they come back and put a higher shine on the woodwork?

* * *

On a tree in a park in Louisville, Kentucky, after a tornado, someone nailed the cover of the book, "Gone with the Wind."

* * *

In Wilkes-Barre, Pennsylvania, a man who was shoveling mud told a *Time* reporter: "Two things I am learning from this disaster. One: a twenty-five cent calendar covers the wall like a $10,000 painting. Two: when your furniture is out on the curb, it doesn't look any different from anybody else's."

APPENDIX B

Questions You've Always Wanted to Ask About MDS — But Were Afraid to Raise Your Voice

1. Who actually are the Mennonites?

The Anabaptist movement started during the Protestant Reformation about 1525 in Switzerland as a protest against the state church. It supported the idea of a free believers' church in which mature people made commitments to Christ and were baptized upon their confession of faith. The Mennonites are named after a former Roman Catholic priest, Menno Simons, in Holland, who espoused the views of the Anabaptists.

The Mennonites and Amish—the latter an offshoot group named for its founder, Jacob Amman—began coming to America from Switzerland and Germany about 1700, at first to Pennsylvania and then spreading to the West. Later waves of Mennonites came to the United States and Canada from Europe, Russia, and even Paraguay. At first they were mostly farmers, but later moved into all occupations.

Some Old Order Amish still do not use cars, electricity, or even lightning rods on their barns. Less conservative Mennonites have adopted modern dress, education, and technology. Most of them refuse to participate in the military and prefer alternate types of service to society. All practice mutual help.

2. Why are there so many different kinds of Mennonites? I think I can name at least a dozen.

Divisions in the church have occurred over both major and minor issues. C. H. Smith in *The Story of the Mennonites* explains that the Mennonite faith has fostered a strong individualism. This spirit may strengthen character but results in a lack of uniformity. Furthermore, the congregational form of government and lack of regular unifying conferences in the early years permitted scattered congregations to develop certain slight differences which became points of dispute.

Because the Mennonites for centuries were a rural people and came from humble and simple walks of life, they were not trained to subordinate nonessentials to the broader and more important aspects of life. To them, everything was important. Not to be disregarded is the fact that stubbornness on the part of certain self-willed individuals of quarrelsome disposition caused divisions also.

Why are there so many divisions? Mostly because Mennonites, like all Christians, are still human. They have a deep desire to become part of a pure church of Christ. They know the Bible takes a firm stand on some issues, and they must too. When led by the Spirit, the result has been growth. When led by the spirit of man, the result has been division.

The groups having representation on the MDS section of MCC include the General Conference Mennonite Church, the Mennonite Church, the Mennonite Brethren, the Conservative Mennonites, the Brethren in Christ, the Evangelical Mennonite Church, the Evangelical Mennonite Mission Conference, the Beachy Amish Mennonite Church, and the Church of God in Christ, Mennonite, and the Lancaster Mennonite Conference.

3. Where do the Church of God in Christ, Mennonite, and the Amish fit into the MDS program?

Both of these groups have their own disaster organizations but occasionally cooperate with MDS, as in the Rapid City project. Both have representatives on the MDS section of MCC.

4. What is MCC? It is mentioned frequently in this book.

Mennonite Central Committee (MCC) is an inter-Mennonite relief agency begun about 1922 to aid famine-stricken Mennonites in Russia (see Chapter 6) and which has since expanded so that it has health, education, and agricultural programs in thirty-eight countries.

5. What is the relationship of MDS to the American Red Cross?

MDS is recognized by the president and Congress as one of three voluntary agencies included in the Federal Disaster Assistance Administration team. The others are American Red Cross by virtue of its congressional charter of 1905 and the Salvation Army.

The Red Cross has a much wider spectrum of activities than MDS. MDS prefers not to compete with other agencies or to duplicate services. It is usually involved in cleanup, salvage, temporary repairs, and rebuilding programs for the elderly, widowed, underinsured, and disadvantaged following a disaster. On some locations, MDS becomes a department of the Red Cross, taking care of certain aspects of the work such as cleanup and repairs, while the Red Cross provides project leaders and volunteers, food services, lodging, and caseworkers.

The Red Cross and MDS work together in an informal relationship in which both organizations recognize each other's abilities and mutual interest in serving disaster victims. MDS regional directors relate with area Red Cross disaster directors. Unit coordinators are acquainted with the sixty-nine Red Cross divisional disaster directors. A number of the more than 3,300 chapter disaster directors of Red Cross are in dialogue with MDS area district and zone contact persons.

6. What about Civil Defense?

The greatest conflict between the desire of MDS volunteers to help and their peace position has occurred with Civil Defense. In the past, MDS was uncertain to what degree cooperation with this organization might require its volunteers to engage in activities they were not ready to perform.

Historically Mennonites are not opposed to helping those suffering from war; they are only opposed to war. Because of a better understanding of Mennonite beliefs,

Civil Defense has become more sensitive to the MDS position in recent years.

7. How does MDS relate to civic agencies?

On occasion, both stateside and overseas, MDS has worked with Lions Clubs International, the only major service organization which includes natural disaster assistance in its program.

8. Do most large denominations have similar disaster organizations to help meet emergency situations?

The Church of the Brethren is the only other denomination with an organized Christian disaster program similar to MDS. The Christian Reformed Church maintains a disaster ministry and has supported MDS on occasion with funds and volunteers. The Apostolic Christian Church also supports MDS with project funding. The mainline denominations such as Baptists, Disciples, Episcopalians, Lutherans, Methodists, and Presbyterians and others are getting involved in various ways in disaster services, some independently, others through the domestic disaster department of Church World Service.

In recent years a number of successful interchurch and interfaith programs have been organized on a local level to launch community disaster recovery projects. The prototype for such a program and projects was possibly the Rapid City, South Dakota, Church Disaster Response.

The large Catholic bodies have developed a Catholic Disaster Relief Committee to cope with natural disaster situations. Evangelical, fundamentalist, and independent denominations and churches often join in the interfaith programs. Jewish groups support certain programs.

The Kentucky Council of Churches, representing thirteen denominations in the state and with Catholic cooperation, has organized its own Interchurch Recovery Program since the 1974 tornadoes, which will act parallel with MDS.

MDS endeavors to cooperate with various groups. It

is first of all a volunteer movement supplied by funds from its own groups to maintain necessary administration.

9. Does MDS maintain any kind of relationship to state and local disaster and emergency offices?

Yes, but this cooperation varies according to the interest and initiative of the MDS state or unit leaders. Local MDS officers are encouraged to become acquainted with their counterparts in county or municipal disaster public agencies. On the state level, this means learning to know the state civil defense director, highway patrol department, state or National Guard or specially appointed officers.

On the local level, it means having good relations with the police chief or sheriff, the county judge or perhaps the city solicitor, or perhaps even a specially staffed department maintained as a public service for such purposes.

10. Do MDS volunteers actually never get paid?

All volunteers, either by the carload, vanload, or busload, participating in short-term projects serve without any kind of financial remuneration. Their transportation costs are paid personally or by their congregations. On long-term projects, workers are sometimes given minimal allowances if they request it.

11. Who pays the expenses of workers who travel to distant sites or to overseas projects?

The MDS national and international organization pays for the travel of appointed project leaders on long-term operations conducted cooperatively with regional, state, or provincial, or local units.

12. Can only Mennonites act as volunteers?

There is no official membership list for MDS other than church rolls. From the earliest days, a number of non-Mennonites have volunteered to participate in MDS projects.

13. How long does MDS continue in any disaster project?

If the work can be finished in one day, that's the limit. If the need is great, MDS will engage in a long-term project until they are no longer needed. After two years and two months and 19,000 volunteer days of donated labor, MDS phased out its flood recovery program in the Corning-Elmira area, which was launched after Hurricane Agnes swept over it on June 23, 1972. A Mennonite church was phased in.

14. Does MDS have any fund-raising drives to which I can contribute? Where can I send a donation?

The Mennonite conferences and MCC (Canada) support the costs of national and international administration at the national and international levels. Regional and unit costs are funded by local congregations. Donations are accepted from non-Mennonite donors, whether individuals, churches, or agencies, to extend or expand a project so that more families or individuals can be helped. Your donation will be gladly received at either of the following addresses:

Mennonite Disaster Service
21 South 12th Street
Akron, Pennsylvania 17501

or

Mennonite Disaster Service
201-1483 Pembina Highway
Winnipeg, Manitoba R3T 2C8

APPENDIX C

Listing of MDS Units by Regions

REGION I

1. Northern New York
2. Western New York
3. Penn-York
4. Eastern Pennsylvania
5. Lancaster Area, Pennsylvania
6. Cumberland Valley, Pennsylvania
7. Western Pennsylvania and Maryland
8. Delmarva Peninsula
9. Tidewater, Virginia
10. Shenandoah Valley, Virginia
11. North Carolina and Eastern Tennessee
12. South Carolina
13. Alabama and Northwest Florida
14. Central and South Florida
15. Puerto Rico
16. New England States
17. Georgia

REGION II

1. Wisconsin
2. Michigan
3. Illinois
4. Indiana and Lower Michigan
5. Western Ohio
6. Eastern Ohio
7. Kentucky and Tennessee
8. Mississippi-Louisiana

REGION III

1. Western Montana
2. Eastern Montana

3. North Dakota
4. Northern Minnesota
5. Minnesota
6. South Dakota
7. Nebraska
8. Iowa
9. Colorado
10. Kansas
11. Missouri
12. Arkansas
13. Oklahoma
14. New Mexico
15. South Texas

REGION IV

1. Western Washington
2. Eastern Washington
3. Oregon
4. Idaho
5. California
6. Arizona

REGION V (CANADA)

Ontario
Manitoba
Saskatchewan
Alberta
British Columbia

INTERNATIONAL

Honduras

APPENDIX D

Mennonite Disaster Service Organizational Chart

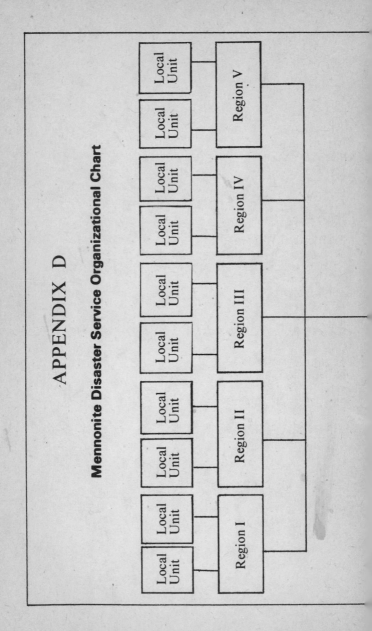

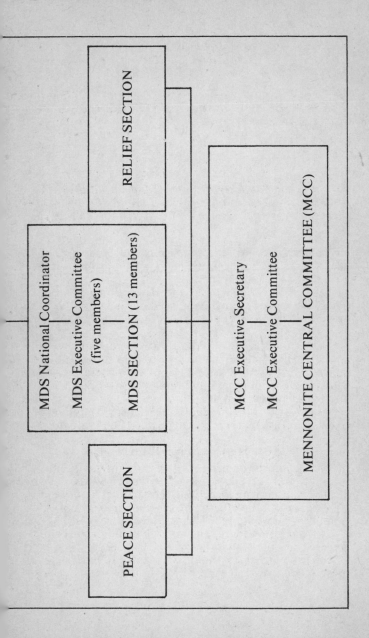

PEACE SECTION

RELIEF SECTION

MDS SECTION (13 members)

MDS Executive Committee (five members)

MDS National Coordinator

MENNONITE CENTRAL COMMITTEE (MCC)

MCC Executive Committee

MCC Executive Secretary

APPENDIX E

The text of two leaflets MDS volunteers distribute.

Why We Are Here

Bear ye one another's burdens, and so fulfill the law of Christ. . . . Thou shalt love the Lord thy God with all thy heart . . . and thy neighbor as thyself. —The Bible

We may be strangers to you but you are our neighbors. We cannot fully understand your loss but we want to share your burden.

We wish to follow Christ and His teaching in all our living. We consider anyone in need our neighbor. When disaster strikes we desire to give assistance as we are able.

God sent Jesus into this world of distress and sin because He understands and wants to help those who are in need. As Christian people we want to share this love with you by helping you and reminding you that Christ died to redeem each of us.

If we can be of further assistance, whether physical or spiritual, please feel free to call on any of our volunteers.

After Disaster, a New Beginning

Once a man stopped to ask a boy how to get to a certain town. The boy knew where the town was, but he had difficulty giving directions. Three times he began to tell the man the turns he should make and the landmarks he would see. Then he gave up.

"If I was going there," he said, "I wouldn't start from here."

You probably think that if you wanted to find the way to God, you wouldn't start with a disaster. I might think so, too. But here we are! Right in the middle of one. And God seems to be far away, and not paying much attention to us.

But wait a minute! Maybe now is just the time to be thinking about Him. We can't control a disaster. We can't control our lives, either, even though we try. We do many things that give us headaches and heartaches afterward. Many times we get our lives so tangled up that they become disaster areas, too, and we don't know where to begin to clean up the mess.

Jesus Christ came to us for just such a time. He said, "I am the way to the Father, the way to God. Believe that I died for your sins, and God will forgive you for My sake."

This is the first step out of personal disaster and toward God, to believe that He will forgive you, and accept you through Jesus.

But don't stop with merely cleaning up the debris in your life! Jesus promised to make the one who comes to Him into a new person.

The Bible explains it this way: "When someone becomes a Christian he becomes a brand-new person inside. He is not the same anymore. A new life has begun! All these new things are from God who brought us back to Himself through what Christ Jesus did."

This new life is a life of joy. But it is not always an easy life. Disasters and disappointments come just as they did before. But the man who has given his life to Christ has faith to stand upon in times of trouble.

"We have gone through many difficulties, but God has kept us through them all. Our hearts ache, but at the same time we have the joy of the Lord. We are poor, but we give rich spiritual gifts to others."

Christ calls His followers to care for each other, and to share with them, for His sake.

"Whatever we do, it is certainly not for our own profit, but because Christ's love controls us now."

A disaster doesn't mean that God is far away. It means instead that He is very near to you, and thinking about you in particular, you personally. He sends many volunteers to help clean up and build again. He sent His only Son to take away your sin and to give you a new life. He wants you to think about Him. And right now is the very time for you to begin thinking seriously about Him, and what He wants to do in your life.

Note: Scripture quoted above is from *The Living Bible.* If you have found reading the Bible difficult, use this version as a study help. It costs only a few dollars and is available in many bookstores.

A more economical version of the entire New Testament is *Good News for Modern Man,* also in modern English. This is available from the American Bible Society or your favorite bookstore.

BIBLIOGRAPHY

For a more thorough introduction to the Mennonites, their faith, life, and work, pick up one or more of the following books at your bookstore:

Books about Mennonites
Bender, H. S. and C. Henry Smith. *Mennonites and Their Heritage.* Scottdale, Pa.: Herald Press, 1964. A handbook of Mennonite history and beliefs for those who want facts in an easy-to-understand form.
Denlinger, Martha A. *Real People: Amish and Mennonites in Lancaster County.* Scottdale, Pa.: Herald Press, 1975.
Dyck, Cornelius J. *An Introduction to Mennonite History: A Popular History of the Anabaptists and Mennonites.* Scottdale, Pa.: Herald Press, 1967.
Epp, Frank H. *Mennonite Exodus: The Rescue and Resettlement of the Russian Mennonites Since the Communist Revolution.* Altona, Man.: D. W. Friesen & Sons, Ltd., 1962.
————.*Mennonites in Canada 1786-1920: The History of a Separate People.* Toronto: MacMillan Company, 1975.
Good, Merle. *These People Mine.* Scottdale, Pa.: Herald Press, 1973.
Hostetler, John A. *Mennonite Life.* Scottdale, Pa.: Herald Press, 1967.
Mennonite Encyclopedia: A Comprehensive Reference Work on the Anabaptist-Mennonite Movement. 4 Volumes. Scottdale, Pa.: Mennonite Publishing House, 1955.
Smith, C. Henry. *The Story of the Mennonites.* Newton, Kan.: Mennonite Publication Office, 1957. An overall treatment of Mennonites in Europe and America in popular style.

Wenger, J. C. *The Mennonite Church in America*. Scottdale, Pa.: Herald Press, 1966.

Inter-Mennonite Publications

Festival Quarterly, a magazine emphasizing Mennonites in the arts, available from 2947 Lincoln Highway East, Lancaster, Pa. 17602.

Mennonite Life, a quarterly magazine, presenting Mennonite principles, doctrines, culture, and history in popular and illustrated form available from Bethel College, North Newton, Kan. 67114.

Mennonite Reporter, an inter-Mennonite Canadian newspaper issued biweekly by Mennonite Publishing Service, Waterloo, Ont. N2L 3G6.

Mennonite Weekly Review, an inter-Mennonite newspaper, published weekly by Herald Publishing Co., 129 West 6th St., Newton, Kan. 67114.

Mennonite Cookbooks

Canadian Mennonite Cookbook (formerly Altona Women's Institute Cookbook). Altona, Man.: D. W. Friesen & Sons, Ltd., 1967.

Kaufman, Edna Ramseyer, Ed. *Melting Pot of Mennonite Cookery, 1874-1974.* North Newton, Kan.: Bethel College Women's Association, 1974.

Longacre, Doris Janzen. *More-with-Less Cookbook.* Scottdale, Pa.: Herald Press, 1976. Commissioned by Mennonite Central Committee in light of world food needs.

The Mennonite Treasury of Recipes. Steinbach, Man.: Canadian Mennonite Conference, 1962.

Schrock, Johnny. *Wonderful Good Cooking.* Scottdale, Pa.: Herald Press, 1975.

Showalter, Mary Emma. *Mennonite Community Cookbook.* Scottdale, Pa.: Herald Press, 1957.

THE AUTHOR

Katie Funk Wiebe was born in northern Saskatchewan of Mennonite Brethren parents who had emigrated from Russia.

Following her husband, Walter's, death in 1962, she determined to complete her formal education and pursue writing. She received her BA from Tabor College, Hillsboro, Kansas, in 1968 and her MA in English from Wichita State University in 1972. She is presently head of the English department at Tabor College.

Mrs. Wiebe has served as a columnist for *Christian Leader* for fourteen years. Her free-lance articles appear widely in the religious press. She is author of a biography of Missionary Paulina Foote, *Have Cart Will Travel,* and coauthor with her late husband of *Youth Worker Programs Helps*, *Study Guide* to David Augsburger's *Freedom of Forgiveness*.

Mrs. Wiebe is the mother of four children: Joanna, Susan (Mrs. Roger Harms), Christine, and James.